HSOAC
HOMELAND SECURITY
OPERATIONAL ANALYSIS CENTER

T0303161

Assessing the Cost of Disaster Recovery and Identifying Funding Sources in the HSOAC Puerto Rico Economic and Disaster Recovery Plan Project

MICHAEL KENNEDY, DAVID METZ, ELAINE K. DEZENSKI, JOSHUA BIRENBAUM, CEDRIC KENNEY

APPROVED FOR PUBLIC RELEASE; DISTRIBUTION UNLIMITED

Published in 2020

Preface

On August 8, 2018, the government of Puerto Rico submitted to the U.S. Congress its economic and disaster recovery plan, as required by the Bipartisan Budget Act of 2018; it was simultaneously published as *Transformation and Innovation in the Wake of Devastation: An Economic and Disaster Recovery Plan for Puerto Rico*.[1] Under contract with the Federal Emergency Management Agency (FEMA), the Homeland Security Operational Analysis Center (HSOAC) provided substantial support in developing the plan by soliciting and integrating inputs from a wide variety of stakeholders, contributing analysis where needed, and assisting with drafting the plan. The plan included an overview of damage and needs, courses of action to meet those needs, costs of the courses of action, and potential funding mechanisms for those costs.

To support federal agencies evaluating and funding recovery actions, HSOAC is releasing this detailed volume on the work done on estimating the cost of the recovery actions included in the plan, as well as on identifying potential funding sources for the recovery actions. HSOAC plans to release another report describing the overall process and methodology employed in this work, an in-depth description of hurricane damage and recovery needs, and detailed volumes for the sectors engaged as part of recovery planning. These volumes will provide decisionmakers greater detail on the conditions in Puerto Rico prior to the 2017 hurricane season, damage from Hurricanes Irma and Maria, courses of action that were identified to help the various sectors (and, more broadly, Puerto Rico) recover in a resilient manner, potential funding mechanisms for the courses of action, and considerations for implementers as they move forward.

This document will likely also be of interest to other stakeholders funding or implementing recovery activities in Puerto Rico, including commonwealth- and local-level governmental agencies, nongovernmental organizations, and the private sector. Furthermore, this body of material contributes to the larger literature about disaster recovery and resilience, and may be of interest to other communities planning for or recovering from similar disasters.

This research was sponsored by FEMA and conducted within the Strategy, Policy, and Operations Program of HSOAC, a federally funded research and development center (FFRDC). More information about HSOAC's contribution to planning for recovery in Puerto Rico, along with links to other reports being published as part of this series, can be found at www.rand.org/hsoac/puerto-rico-recovery.

[1] Government of Puerto Rico, *Transformation and Innovation in the Wake of Devastation: An Economic and Disaster Recovery Plan for Puerto Rico*, San Juan, P.R.: Government of Puerto Rico, August 8, 2018.

About the Homeland Security Operational Analysis Center

The Homeland Security Act of 2002 (Section 305 of Public Law 107-296, as codified at 6 U.S.C. 185), authorizes the Secretary of Homeland Security, acting through the Under Secretary for Science and Technology, to establish one or more FFRDCs to provide independent analysis of homeland security issues. The RAND Corporation operates HSOAC as an FFRDC for the U.S. Department of Homeland Security (DHS) under contract HSHQDC-16-D-00007.

HSOAC provides the government with independent and objective analyses and advice in core areas important to the department in support of policy development, decisionmaking, alternative approaches, and new ideas on issues of significance. HSOAC also works with and supports other federal, state, local, tribal, and public- and private-sector organizations that make up the homeland security enterprise. HSOAC's research is undertaken by mutual consent with DHS and is organized as a set of discrete tasks. This report presents the results of research and analysis conducted under Task Order 70FBR218F00000032, Puerto Rico Economic and Disaster Recovery Plan: Integration and Analytic Support.

The results presented in this report do not necessarily reflect official DHS opinion or policy.

For more information on HSOAC, see www.rand.org/hsoac.

For more information on this publication, visit www.rand.org/t/RR2861.

Contents

Figures

Tables

Summary

On September 19 and 20, 2017, Hurricane Maria caused widespread destruction across Puerto Rico. Making landfall just two weeks after Hurricane Irma, Maria—a strong Category 4 storm—significantly damaged local infrastructure and interrupted the provision of essential services to the people of Puerto Rico. Attention has now turned toward Puerto Rico's long-term recovery needs. A supplemental appropriations bill passed by the U.S. Congress on February 8, 2018, required the governor of Puerto Rico, in coordination with the Federal Emergency Management Agency (FEMA), the Department of the Treasury, the Department of Energy, and other federal agencies with responsibilities under the National Disaster Recovery Framework,[1] to submit a report to Congress within 180 days of enactment of the legislation that described Puerto Rico's economic and disaster recovery plan.

The government of Puerto Rico's *Transformation and Innovation in the Wake of Devastation: An Economic and Disaster Recovery Plan for Puerto Rico* was published in August 2018, and lays out the priorities, goals, and expected outcomes of the recovery effort.[2] FEMA asked the Homeland Security Operational Analysis Center (HSOAC) to provide analytical support to the government of Puerto Rico in its formulation of the recovery plan.[3]

Governor Ricardo Rosselló's plan for recovery includes a set of 276 courses of action (COAs). A COA is an activity, policy, program, or strategy designed to further the goals of the recovery plan. Each individual COA is a recovery activity designed to redress the hurricane damage and preexisting economic needs faced by Puerto Rico. COAs were organized into portfolios developed around nine capital investments and eight strategic initiatives identified by the government of Puerto Rico. The capital investments were further divided into three priority areas: physical capital, human capital, and natural capital. The strategic initiatives "build on the nine fundamental capital investments and capitalize on Puerto Rico's unique assets and strengths to promote economic growth that is grounded in innovation, sustainability, and resilience."[4] Several portfolios were developed for each capital investment and strategic initiative, and represented different approaches and levels of effort in achieving that investment or initiative. The government of Puerto Rico, represented by the governor and his staff, selected which of

---

[1] U.S. Department of Homeland Security (DHS), *National Disaster Recovery Framework*, 2nd ed., Washington, D.C.: DHS, 2016.

[2] Government of Puerto Rico, 2018.

[3] More information about HSOAC's contribution to planning for recovery in Puerto Rico, along with links to other reports being published as part of this series, can be found at RAND Corporation, "Supporting Puerto Rico's Disaster-Recovery Planning," webpage, undated.

[4] Government of Puerto Rico, 2018, page xii; the nine capital investments and eight strategic initiatives are further defined on page xiii.

these portfolios, and thus which COAs, to include in the recovery plan, using a decision support tool developed by HSOAC. The capital investments and strategic initiatives are listed in Table S.1. Figure 1.1 in the appendix to Chapter 1 provides more detail on them.

Table S.1. Capital Investments and Strategic Initiatives in Puerto Rico's Recovery Plan

	Priority Area	Capital Investment or Strategic Initiative
Capital Investments	Physical capital	Energy
		Communications and information technology
		Water
		Transportation
		Housing
		Public buildings
	Human capital	Education
		Health and well-being
	Natural capital	Natural environment
Strategic Initiatives		Ocean economy (BLUEtide Initiative[a])
		Visitor economy
		Emergency services modernization
		Agricultural transformation
		Digital transformation
		21st-century workforce
		Entrepreneurship
		Advanced manufacturing

NOTE: [a] The BLUEtide Initiative is "an interdisciplinary collaborative approach to draft an economic recovery strategy for island states and territories, anchored in a blue economy framework." See BLUEtide Initiative, homepage, undated.

Many COAs were included in several capital investment and/or strategic initiative portfolios, so the analytical work for the plan was organized around 12 sectors, each with its own sector analysis team. The sector structure was a partition of the COAs—that is, each COA was a member of one and only one sector. Thus, sector costs aggregate to total cost of the recovery plan with no double counting, which would not be true of portfolio costs.

This report describes the work done on estimating the costs of the COAs, and on identifying potential funding sources for each COA. The primary challenge of the cost analysis was the sheer diversity of the activities included in the plan. Due to the substantial number of COAs, their sectoral specificity, the technical complexity of infrastructure and other investments, and the great diversity of activities involved, a decentralized approach was used to estimate the cost of the COAs, with direction by expert-led sector teams and overall guidance and review provided by a small central team of cost analysts. To ensure consistency across the sector team estimates, we developed general ground rules for cost estimation. These included broadly dividing costs into *upfront* and *recurring* costs, selecting a common time horizon for estimating costs, estimating all costs in constant dollar terms, and, where feasible, using standard unit costs—such as labor rates, construction and materials costs, and operations and maintenance costs.

In this report we illustrate many of the complexities associated with estimating the costs of a recovery plan. In practical terms, actual cost estimates may have to be done in a simpler way because data, or time and resources, do not exist to support more detailed estimation. This is illustrated with examples of our cost estimation for Puerto Rico's recovery plan.

Table S.2 lists the sectors included in the recovery plan, along with the cost for each sector. The total estimated cost of the plan is $139 billion, which includes $105 billion in upfront costs and $34 billion in recurring costs.

Table S.2. Recovery Plan Costs by Sector (in billions of 2018 dollars)

Sector	Upfront Cost	Recurring Cost	Total Cost
Communications and Information Technology	1.9	1.3	3.2
Community Planning and Capacity Building	0.1	0.5	0.6
Economics	6.1	0.2	6.3
Education	7.7	7.5	15.2
Energy	15.0	11.0	26.0
Health and Social Services	5.3	1.0	6.3
Housing	30.1	2.5	32.6
Municipalities	0.05	0.1	0.2
Natural and Cultural Resources	3.5	0.4	3.9
Public Buildings	5.1	0.7	5.8
Transportation	6.3	2.1	8.4
Water	23.5	6.4	30.0
TOTAL	104.6	33.9	138.5

This report considers three levels of detail in funding analysis: First, it identifies potential funding sources and the dollar value of their contribution to the recovery plan. Second, it identifies specific potential funding sources for each COA. And third, it discusses construction of a complete funding plan, which would identify specific funders and their contribution to each COA.

The potential funding sources we identify include both sources with estimated funding amounts and sources for which no dollar-value estimate of their contribution to Puerto Rico's recovery is currently available. The primary funding sources whose funding levels could be estimated include federal government sources and proceeds from private insurance. Federal government sources include the Disaster Relief Fund (DRF), other appropriations made for disaster relief in legislation, and regular ongoing federal programs. Table S.3 lists these sources, along with their estimated contributions to the recovery plan. The total amount of potential funding from these sources is $93.6 billion. Of this, $85.6 billion is from the federal government. In addition, the government of Puerto Rico projects that $8 billion will be available in proceeds from private insurance. Because the estimated cost of the plan is $139 billion, and estimated funding is $93.6 billion, at least a $45.4 billion gap remains. Should any of the federal funds shown in Table S.3 ultimately not materialize, the gap would be concomitantly larger. If the plan is to be fully implemented, additional sources to fund this gap must be found.

Table S.3. Funding Sources, with Estimates of Funding Levels

Funding Source	Estimated Level (in billions of 2018 dollars)
DRF individual assistance	0.8
DRF public assistance	37.4
DRF Hazard Mitigation Grant Program	3.0
Non-DRF appropriations: CDBG-DR	19.9
Non-DRF appropriations: other	21.2
Regular federal programs	3.3
Private insurance	8.0
TOTAL	93.6

Figure S.1 shows potential federal agency funding sources by sector. The shaded cells indicate an agency may be a potential funder for any COA in the sector.

Some funders, particularly certain federal programs, will fund only a percentage of any project and require a matching contribution. As such, many COAs will necessarily have more than one funder.

A very high level (99.2 percent) of the $139 billion total cost of the recovery plan is *eligible* for federal funding. But since only $85.6 billion of potential federal funding has been identified, the $45.4 billion gap between the estimate of federal funding (plus insurance proceeds) and the funding required to fully implement the recovery plan remains (along with any portion of the federal funds that we estimate available for Puerto Rico's recovery that may not ultimately materialize).

Figure S.1. Potential Federal Funding Sources, by Sector

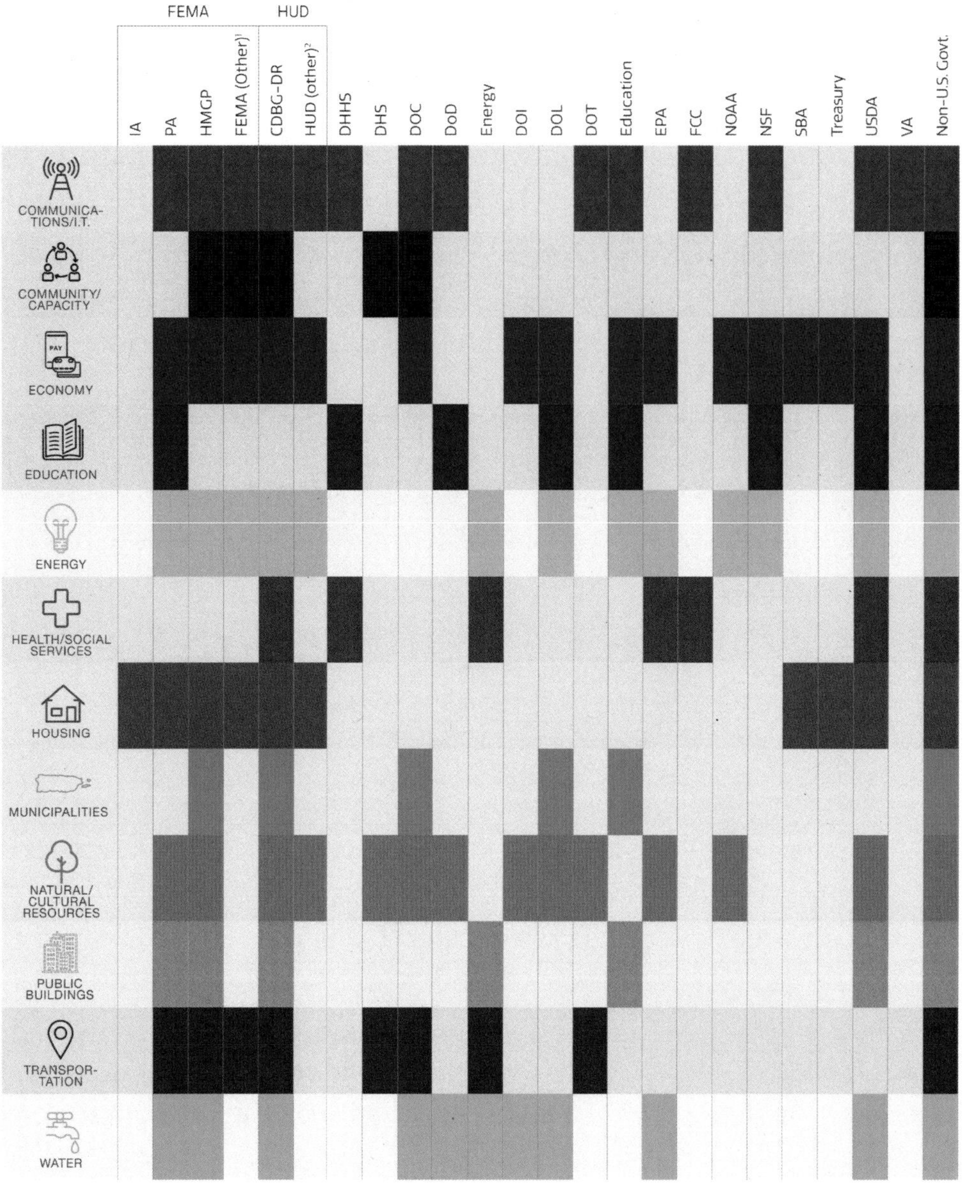

1. FEMA (other) includes the National Flood Insurance Program, Emergency Management Performance Grant, Dislocated Workers Program, port security grants, and the Pre-Disaster Mitigation Program, among others.
2. HUD (other) includes the CDBG Entitlement Program, Capital Fund Program, Rental Assistance Demonstration Program, Choice Neighborhoods Program, Section 18 (Demolition/Disposal), Energy Performance Contracting, and Housing Choice Voucher Program, among others.

SOURCE: Government of Puerto Rico, 2018, p. 170.

This report identifies other potential sources of funding from which the remaining $45.4 billion might potentially be found. Additional funding contributions will come from Puerto Rican governmental entities, at either the commonwealth or municipal level, and proceeds from COAs that are revenue-generating projects. However, the contribution from these sources is currently uncertain.

Potential contributions can also be had from nongovernmental sources, such as private-sector funding and philanthropic actors, although their amount is also currently uncertain. Some private investors already figure prominently in natural disaster response, recovery, and mitigation. Public-private partnerships can be a viable way of injecting immediate resources into much-needed infrastructure projects, adding financial flexibility and bringing corporate innovation and technology. While philanthropic actors will not cover most of the costs, they may identify specific needs that align with their interests and capabilities to make a meaningful contribution to Puerto Rico's recovery. These include contributions from charitable foundations, corporate foundations, individual donations, and local and international nongovernmental organizations.

Finally, we discuss construction of a complete funding plan, which would identify specific funders and their contribution to each COA. We judged, and FEMA concurred, that constructing such a plan would not be useful at this early stage of the recovery process. One reason is the large gap between estimated plan cost and the funding amounts currently identified. Allocating the funding available would necessarily fund only a subset of the total plan, which would require an assessment (at least implicit) of the relative value of COAs. We had no basis on which do so; the plan was designed as an integral whole.

We do describe a formal programming approach to funding analysis that addresses two questions: Is there an allocation of funders to COAs so that all COA costs are covered? And, if not, what is the best option, given a value function over COA achievement (i.e., amount spent, by cost type, on each COA)? We expect that this approach would be a useful tool as the plan is being implemented in the future.

Acknowledgments

We acknowledge the steadfast support and encouragement of our project sponsor, Michael Byrne, acting Caribbean Area Division director for the Federal Emergency Management Agency (FEMA) and the federal coordinating officer and federal disaster recovery coordinator for Hurricane Irma and Hurricane Maria response and recovery in Puerto Rico. We also acknowledge with gratitude the contributions of other key FEMA partners, including Brian D. Applebee, Sr., finance and administration section chief of the FEMA National Incident Management Assistance Team East 1; Zoe Armstrong, Anne L. Heald, and Andrew R. Slaten, all of FEMA's Hub of Philanthropic Engagement; Luis Avila, Hazard Mitigation Grant Program lead for the Major Disaster Declaration for Hurricane Maria (DR-4339-PR); Gerilee Bennett, director of the Interagency Coordination Division, Field Operations Directorate, Office of Response and Recovery; Paul Bratton, National Disaster Recovery Support (NDRS) Recovery Coordination Task Force leader for interagency recovery coordination, DHS/FEMA/NDRS, DR-4339-PR; Troy J. Notaro, National Spend Plan coordinator, financial management specialist, FEMA National Spend Plan Team; Jon Reistroffer, deputy finance and administration section chief for DR-4339-PR; Toney N. Sanders, Region IV Spend Plan administrator, FEMA National Spend Plan Team; Kevin Snyder, federal disaster recovery coordinator for FEMA Region III; and Hope Thompson of the Office of Policy and Program Analysis.

We owe a special debt of gratitude to Scott Davis, Community Planning and Capacity Building Sector adviser for DR-4339-PR, who was our primary point of FEMA coordination on funding issues. We are also grateful to the many other U.S. government personnel or advisers who gave us very helpful advice and assistance, including Alejandro Contreras, director of preparedness, communication and coordination in the Office of Disaster Assistance, Small Business Administration; Greg Eaton, then of Deloitte Advisory and now of EY; and Johann Sasso, civil engineer, U.S. Army Corps of Engineers.

From the government of Puerto Rico, we are particularly grateful for the inputs of Omar Marrero Diaz and Laura Femenias Jove, the director and associate director of the Central Office of Recovery, Reconstruction, and Resiliency.

Our work on nongovernmental sources of disaster recovery funding was very helpfully informed by discussions with Andy Andrea, founder and executive director of Alliance4Impact; Nick Bailey, vice president for innovation and products at Salesforce.org; Eric Berseth, founder and managing partner of Philanthropy Advisors; Samuel Carter, director and resilience Accelerator of 100 Resilient Cities; Rahul Chandran, executive director of the Global Alliance for Humanitarian Innovation; Petra Demarin; Howard Kunreuther, professor and codirector of the Risk Management and Decision Processes Center, Wharton School, University of Pennsylvania; Gary Lynch, Founder and CEO of the Risk Project; Sergio Marxuach, policy director of the Center for the New Economy; and Josh Sawislak, professional affiliate at the Center for Urban and Environmental Solutions, Florida Atlantic University.

Our RAND Corporation colleagues Rob Leonard and Fred Timson, both seasoned cost analysts, worked with various members of the sector teams to formulate and strengthen their cost estimates; this report is significantly better because of their contributions. Our RAND colleagues Gabriela Castro, Blas Nuñez-Neto, and Chris Schnaubelt were particularly helpful in working with various persons in Puerto Rico. We also gratefully acknowledge the contribution of our RAND colleague Jeremy Eckhause, who independently developed an approach to funding allocation similar to ours; we have freely drawn from his work. RAND colleagues Joie Acosta and Lloyd Dixon made significant contributions to the nongovernmental funding work.

The authors of this report were part of a much larger project team. The analysis contained here benefited from—and in many cases is directly based on—data collection and analysis by all members of the team. They can be found as authors of the many reports from this project, available at www.rand.org/hsoac/puerto-rico-recovery.

We are particularly grateful to our project leader, Cynthia Cook, who led this large and complex effort with extraordinary intellectual and administrative prowess.

Finally, we would like to thank our peer reviewers, Debra Knopman of RAND and David Kaufman of the Center for Naval Analyses. Their reviews contributed greatly to improving this report.

Abbreviations

ARECMA	Asociación Recreativa y Educativa Comunal Barrio Mariana, Inc.
BAU	business as usual
CDBG-DR	Community Development Block Grant–Disaster Recovery
COA	course of action
CONUS	continental United States
DHHS	U.S. Department of Health and Human Services
DHS	U.S. Department of Homeland Security
DOC	U.S. Department of Commerce
DoD	U.S. Department of Defense
DOI	U.S. Department of the Interior
DOL	U.S. Department of Labor
DOT	U.S. Department of Transportation
DRF	Disaster Relief Fund
DST	decision support tool
EPA	Environmental Protection Agency
FCC	Federal Communications Commission
FEMA	Federal Emergency Management Agency
FFRDC	federally funded research and development center
FY	fiscal year
GDP	gross domestic product
HMGP	Hazard Mitigation Grant Program
HSOAC	Homeland Security Operational Analysis Center
HUD	U.S. Department of Housing and Urban Development
IA	individual assistance
NDRS	National Disaster Recovery Support
NGO	nongovernmental organization
NOAA	National Oceanic and Atmospheric Administration

NSF	National Science Foundation
O&M	operations and maintenance
PA	public assistance
P3	public-private partnership
SBA	Small Business Administration
SME	subject matter expert
SWF	sovereign wealth fund
USDA	U.S. Department of Agriculture
VA	U.S. Department of Veterans Affairs

1. Introduction

The Background to This Work

On September 19–20, 2017, Hurricane Maria caused widespread destruction across Puerto Rico. Making landfall just two weeks after Hurricane Irma, Maria—a strong Category 4 storm—significantly damaged local infrastructure and interrupted the provision of essential services to the people of Puerto Rico. On September 20, 2017, President Donald J. Trump signed a Major Disaster Declaration for Hurricane Maria, DR-4339, under the Robert T. Stafford Disaster Relief and Emergency Assistance Act.

For more than a decade before the hurricanes struck, Puerto Rico had been grappling with an economic crisis. Structural changes in demography, social stresses, deterioration of infrastructure, and significant numbers of people leaving Puerto Rico combined to exacerbate the impact of the hurricanes.

On February 8, 2018, in response to the damage wrought by Hurricanes Irma and Maria, Congress enacted H.R. 1892 as Public Law 115-123, the Bipartisan Budget Act of 2018. This act required the governor of Puerto Rico, in coordination with the Federal Emergency Management Agency (FEMA), the U.S. Department of the Treasury, the U.S. Department of Energy, and other federal agencies with responsibilities under the National Disaster Recovery Framework,[1] to submit a report to Congress within 180 days that described Puerto Rico's 12- and 24-month economic and disaster recovery plan. The act mandated that the recovery plan define "the priorities, goals, and expected outcomes of the recovery effort for the Commonwealth based on damage assessments prepared pursuant to Federal law, if applicable" for economic issues, electric power systems and grid restoration, environmental issues, governance and civic institutions, health and social services, housing, natural and cultural resources, and other infrastructure systems. The resulting recovery plan, *Transformation and Innovation in the Wake of Devastation: An Economic and Disaster Recovery Plan for Puerto Rico*, is intended to provide Puerto Rico a path toward economic sustainability, growth, and resilience as it reconstructs and recovers from the impact of Hurricanes Irma and Maria.[2] FEMA asked the Homeland Security Operational Analysis Center (HSOAC) to develop an information base that would inform the development of this recovery plan by the government of Puerto Rico. This report summarizes specifically the

[1] U.S. Department of Homeland Security (DHS), *National Disaster Recovery Framework*, 2nd ed., Washington, D.C.: DHS, 2016.

[2] Government of Puerto Rico, 2018.

cost and funding work that HSOAC used to support the government of Puerto Rico in its development of the recovery plan.[3]

The HSOAC team solicited feedback from external subject matter experts (SMEs) and stakeholders in Puerto Rico, assessed damage and recovery needs by sector, clarified priorities, identified and evaluated potential solutions, estimated rough-order-of-magnitude costs, and identified potential funding sources for an array of courses of action (COAs), which are recovery activities designed to redress the hurricane damage and preexisting economic needs faced by Puerto Rico. This iterative and collaborative planning process provided the basis for developing the recovery plan, with the final decisions on the content of the plan made by the governor of Puerto Rico, not HSOAC. This report is intended to give the reader insight into the methodology behind the cost and funding part of the recovery planning process.

Cost and Funding Analysis in Development of the Recovery Plan

The government of Puerto Rico's *Transformation and Innovation in the Wake of Devastation: An Economic and Disaster Recovery Plan for Puerto Rico* includes a set of 276 COAs.[4] COAs are organized into portfolios developed around nine capital investments and eight strategic initiatives identified by the government of Puerto Rico. The capital investments are further divided into three Priority Areas: Physical Capital, Human Capital, and Natural Capital. The strategic initiatives "build on the nine fundamental capital investments and capitalize on Puerto Rico's unique assets and strengths to promote economic growth that is grounded in innovation, sustainability, and resilience."[5] Several portfolios were developed for each capital investment and strategic initiative, and they represented different approaches and levels of effort in achieving the investment or initiative. The government of Puerto Rico, represented by the governor and his staff, selected which of these portfolios, and thus which COAs, were included in the recovery plan, using a decision support tool (DST) developed by HSOAC. The nine capital investments and eight strategic initiatives are listed in Table 1.1. Figure 1.1 in the appendix to this chapter provides more detail on them.

---

[3] For more information about HSOAC's contribution to planning for recovery in Puerto Rico, along with links to other reports being published as part of this series, see RAND Corporation, undated.

[4] Government of Puerto Rico, 2018.

[5] Government of Puerto Rico, 2018, p. xii; the nine capital investments and eight strategic initiatives are further defined on p. xiii. To elaborate, capital investments include physical, human, and natural capital needed to achieve the goals outlined in the recovery plan. Strategic initiatives, which build on the robust infrastructure recovery made possible by the capital investments, are sets of actions aimed at driving Puerto Rico's future in specific ways consistent with Governor Ricardo Rosselló's vision. The strategic initiatives are crosscutting initiatives to build resilience, improve society, and grow the economy; they also reflect aspirational directions for Puerto Rico's future. More detail on this can be found at Government of Puerto Rico, 2018, pp. xii–xiii.

Table 1.1. Capital Investments and Strategic Initiatives in Puerto Rico's Recovery Plan

	Priority Area	Capital Investment or Strategic Initiative
Capital Investments	Physical capital	Energy
		Communications and information technology
		Water
		Transportation
		Housing
		Public buildings
	Human capital	Education
		Health and well-being
	Natural capital	Natural environment
Strategic Initiatives		Ocean economy (BLUEtide Initiative[a])
		Visitor economy
		Emergency services modernization
		Agricultural transformation
		Digital transformation
		21st-century workforce
		Entrepreneurship
		Advanced manufacturing

NOTE: [a] The BLUEtide Initiative is "an interdisciplinary collaborative approach to draft an economic recovery strategy for island states and territories, anchored in a blue economy framework." See BLUEtide Initiative, homepage, undated.

Many COAs were included in several capital investment and/or strategic initiative portfolios, so the analytical work for the plan was organized around 12 recovery sectors. The sector structure was a partition of the COAs—that is, each COA was a member of one and only one sector. Thus, sector costs aggregate to total plan cost with no double counting, which would not be true of portfolio costs. The 12 sectors were designed to complement the National Disaster Recovery Framework sectors,[6] which include Community Planning and Capacity Building, Economics, Housing, Health and Social Services, Infrastructure Systems, and Natural and Cultural Resources. For the Puerto Rico recovery effort, a Municipalities Sector was added, and the sectors for Health and Social Services and Infrastructure Systems were further divided to provide a manageable research scope for each team. The 12 resulting sectors were

- Communications and Information Technology
- Community Planning and Capacity Building
- Economics
- Education
- Energy
- Health and Social Services

[6] DHS, 2016.

- Housing
- Municipalities
- Natural and Cultural Resources
- Public Buildings
- Transportation
- Water.

To support the recovery analysis effort, HSOAC organized into 12 sector analysis teams, working in partnership with FEMA's Recovery Support Functions solutions-based teams, FEMA's sector teams, the government of Puerto Rico, and other local partners and stakeholders. These partnered teams identified a large number of potential COAs for each sector; the government of Puerto Rico, represented by Governor Ricardo Rosselló and his staff, ultimately selected which COAs were included in the final plan.

This was done with the support of HSOAC's DST, which offered a summary visualization of alternative choices and their impact on total plan cost.[7] First, government of Puerto Rico personnel, working with HSOAC, identified the set of nine capital investments and eight strategic initiatives for Puerto Rico's economic and disaster recovery. The partnered teams then developed the set of portfolios for each of these investments and initiatives; these portfolios are simply collections of COAs organized around a recovery theme. Each portfolio represented a different level of effort in achieving the capital investment and strategic initiative goals. Some portfolios were minimal—for example, just repairing what was broken by the hurricanes. Others included a focus on resilience. And some portfolios included additional investments whose goal is to change the future of Puerto Rico by building a stronger and more viable economy. Using the DST, the government of Puerto Rico, represented by the governor and his staff, then selected which portfolios, and thus what COAs, to include in the final plan. Ultimately, 276 COAs were included in the plan.

Part of the information presented through the DST to the government of Puerto Rico personnel doing portfolio selection was the estimated cost of the COAs in each portfolio and their potential funding sources. While the cost information was given to government of Puerto Rico personnel, no specific budget constraint was imposed. Thus, they made decisions unconstrained by any particular numerical budget but were fully cognizant of the cost estimates. They were free to choose more comprehensive—and thus more effective but also more costly—portfolios, knowing that a more costly plan implied a more difficult funding challenge. The plan ultimately chosen thus reflected their judgment balancing plan comprehensiveness versus funding difficulty.

As stated above, we characterize our cost estimates as rough-order-of-magnitude estimates. These cost estimates have two roles in recovery plan development. First, once the plan is finalized, the cost estimates inform policymakers of the level of resources needed to implement it. Second, COA-specific cost estimates and cross-COA comparisons can directly support prioritization of resources, as in the portfolio selection approach to plan development used in this

[7] For additional information on the methods used to develop the recovery plan, see RAND Corporation, undated.

case. A caveat on these cost estimates, however, is that they are intended only to support high-level planning—in particular, to inform decisionmakers as they balance costs against expected benefits in selecting COAs. They are not meant to be bid-quality estimates. In fact, some COA costs in the recovery plan are given as both a point estimate and a range in order to emphasize the uncertainty inherent in the estimates at this stage of recovery analysis. The range might reflect, for example, uncertainty about the cost of equipment, materials, or labor, or about the current number and condition of structures that will be repaired or rebuilt. The costs reported here are the point estimates. We judge that such rough-order-of-magnitude estimates are appropriate to support plan *development*. For plan *execution*, much better cost estimates—based on actual plans for construction projects, government activities, and the like—are required, but they were beyond the scope of this work.

In the Appendix to Chapter 2 we describe some potential extensions to our cost analysis that we did not have time or resources available to carry out—in particular, the estimation of how absorptive capacity constraints might affect cost. Based on discussions with knowledgeable persons, we assessed that absorptive capacity cost pressures would offset the overall lower level of construction costs in Puerto Rico, and our estimates are based on this. If the first of these factors outweighs the second, our estimates will be correspondingly high, and vice versa. This is one example in which our planning-quality cost estimates are certainly not of bid quality. But we assess that they are appropriate for developing the plan, in that the extra time required to further refine the cost estimates would not justify the resulting delay in plan formulation. As plan implementation moves forward, the cost estimate for each COA should be improved as more sector- and project-specific information is collected and analyzed.

The Organization of This Report

Chapter 2 describes the scope of the cost estimation work, which required estimating the cost of a remarkably diverse set of activities. It presents the ground rules used in cost estimation and gives a general overview of how the cost estimates were developed. The chapter also presents an important distinction between two broad categories of costs: *upfront* costs (those that are incurred once in the course of implementing or carrying out a COA, and never again) and *recurring* costs (those that are incurred regularly over the course of the recovery plan). Chapter 2 discusses other subcategories of costs estimated, and presents methodological options we considered and why we made the decisions we did on methodology. It goes into detail on some examples of kinds of COAs whose costs we estimated. One example is costing COAs whose primary costs were personnel related, and we present some discussion of estimating personnel costs. The chapter then summarizes our findings on cost, including our overall estimate of $139 billion for the cost of the recovery plan, of which $105 billion is upfront cost and $34 billion is recurring cost.

The **Appendix to Chapter 2** presents a more formal approach to cost analysis. It discusses how COAs might be categorized as indivisible or divisible. That is, they may be *binary*, so that they have value only if fully implemented, or they be *continuous*, so that they can be usefully carried out at different levels. It then discusses how recurring costs may be related to upfront costs for many COAs, particularly if the upfront costs represent building or repairing some facility and recurring costs represent operating it. The level of recurring costs will then depend on how upfront costs are incurred over time. The appendix also discusses the absorptive capacity issue—that is, that input costs may rise if a large number of recovery activities are undertaken at the same time. It presents a way to incorporate absorptive capacity considerations into cost analysis.

Chapter 3 discusses the funding issue, and describes a number of potential funding sources for Puerto Rico's recovery. For some, we can make estimates of the amount available to Puerto Rico based on legislation or other sources; for others, such as Puerto Rico's own contribution, private investment, or philanthropic funding, we have no analytical base to make an estimate of ultimate dollar amounts, but we identify them as potential sources. We note that the sources whose levels we can estimate do not fully meet the requirements of the recovery plan: these potential sources total $94 billion, compared with the plan's $139 billion total cost. We also discuss the issue of matching funders to COAs. We note that almost all COAs are eligible for federal funding, and we identify potential federal agency funders for each sector.

The **Appendix to Chapter 3** presents a more formal approach to matching funders to COAs, formulated as a mathematical program.

Chapter 4 presents a summation and conclusions.

Chapter Summary

This chapter has provided context for the cost and funding analysis used to support the development of Puerto Rico's recovery plan in the wake of the devastation of Hurricanes Irma and Maria. The impact of that devastation was compounded by an economic crisis in Puerto Rico that spanned more than a decade. To support the effort, HSOAC organized into 12 sector analysis teams, working in partnership with FEMA's Recovery Support Functions solutions-based teams, FEMA's sector teams, the government of Puerto Rico, and other local partners and stakeholders. These partnered teams developed potential COAs for each sector. The government of Puerto Rico, represented by the governor and his staff, selected which COAs were included in the final recovery plan. We described the COA development and selection process in this chapter and discussed how cost and funding information was used in the process. We also discussed how the planning-quality, rough-order-of-magnitude costs estimated for the recovery plan differ from the kind of bid-quality cost estimates required for effective plan execution. Finally, we outlined the contents of the remainder of this report, which covers both the estimation of the costs of the COAs and the identification of potential funding sources for each.

Appendix to Chapter 1: Definitions of Capital Investments and Strategic Initiatives

Figure 1.1 gives broader definitions of capital investments and strategic initiatives.

Figure 1.1. Capital Investments and Strategic Initiatives

CAPITAL INVESTMENTS

Physical Capital

ENERGY

Transform the energy system to ensure customer-centric, affordable, reliable, and scalable electricity that incorporates more renewables, microgrids, and distributed energy resources; can drive new businesses and employment opportunities; and can support residents' well-being.

COMMUNICATIONS/INFORMATION TECHNOLOGY

Modernize the telecommunications system to ensure fast, reliable, and resilient residential, commercial, and emergency communications that drive Puerto Rico's economy, prosperity, and well-being.

WATER

Rethink water systems to be safer, more reliable, and protected from future disasters to ensure the well-being of Puerto Ricans and the environment as well as the operations of government and businesses.

TRANSPORTATION

Rebuild and strengthen maritime, surface, and air transportation to ensure a flexible and reliable transportation system that moves people and goods, ensures economic continuity, and facilitates disaster response.

HOUSING

Repair and rebuild resilient residential housing that is safe and affordable to create a better built environment.

PUBLIC BUILDINGS

Repair, rebuild, and right-size the public buildings inventory to ensure stronger and more resilient public buildings that meet today's standards, mitigate against future disasters, represent innovative designs, and meet communities' needs.

Human Capital

EDUCATION

Transform the education system to produce competitive graduates with the knowledge and skills needed to adapt to changes in the economy, the environment, and technology.

HEALTH AND WELL-BEING

Rebuild and enhance health and social service infrastructure and regional health care networks to ensure reliable and equitable access to health and social services and health-promoting communities, including an efficient and effective response to public health crises and other future disasters.

Natural Capital

NATURAL ENVIRONMENT

Restore, plan for, and develop the natural environment so that marine and terrestrial ecosystems coexist sustainably with tourism, promote the economic development of Puerto Rico, serve as natural infrastructure to protect against storm damage, manage waste, and preserve the natural and cultural heritage of Puerto Ricans.

STRATEGIC INITIATIVES

OCEAN ECONOMY (BLUEtide)

Integrate and promote all of Puerto Rico's ocean-dependent industries and ecosystems as a cohesive effort to promote economic growth, improve quality of life for residents, and enhance the visitor's experience.

VISITOR ECONOMY

Develop a strong visitor economy to help position Puerto Rico as a global destination of investment, production, and wealth.

EMERGENCY SERVICES MODERNIZATION

Enhance public safety and first responders' ability to deliver reliable, modern, and integrated emergency services.

AGRICULTURAL TRANSFORMATION

Modernize agriculture to promote greater productivity and output and improve exports.

DIGITAL TRANSFORMATION

Build the capabilities and workforce needed to fundamentally transform key industry and government processes to become more user-focused, relevant, and efficient at addressing local needs and delivering basic services.

21ST-CENTURY WORKFORCE

Develop and protect human capital to establish a world-class workforce, increase labor force flexibility, and create high-quality employment opportunities aligned with economic growth strategies.

ENTREPRENEURSHIP

Expand opportunities for entrepreneurship and development of small to medium local businesses that can compete globally to promote economic development.

ADVANCED MANUFACTURING

Address policy and structural barriers to increase opportunities for investment and the growth of private-public partnerships.

SOURCE: Government of Puerto Rico, 2018, p. xiii.

2. Estimating the Cost of the Recovery Plan

An Overview of the Cost Estimation Approach

The primary challenge of the cost analysis was the sheer number and diversity of activities included in the recovery plan. The goal of the costing work was to estimate costs consistently across the 276 COAs so that the relative resource challenges of the various COAs were faithfully represented—that is, so that subsequent analysis and selection of COAs for portfolios could be done on a consistent cost basis. We have already discussed how these cost estimates should be interpreted as of planning quality—appropriate for recovery plan development—as opposed to bid quality.

In this section we give a general overview of how cost estimates were developed. We begin with our key ground rules for cost estimation, whose goal was to ensure consistency of the estimates. We divided costs into two broad categories: *upfront* costs (those that are incurred once in the course of implementing or carrying out a COA, and never again) and *recurring* costs (those that are incurred regularly over the course of the recovery plan). We then selected a common time horizon for estimating COA costs: an 11-year period, from fiscal year (FY) 2018 to FY 2028, inclusive. This time horizon was chosen to align with that of the estimate of the Financial Oversight and Management Board of Puerto Rico of recovery *resources* available.[1] All costs were estimated in dollars of 2018 purchasing power, and future costs were not discounted.[2] Where feasible, we used standard unit costs—such as labor rates, construction and materials costs, and operations and maintenance (O&M) costs. We only included costs specifically associated with the recovery plan—that is, costs above and beyond those that would have been incurred in the absence of the disaster ("business as usual," or BAU, costs). This was to ensure that existing activities, for which funds were allocated in the past, were not conflated with new recovery activities, which require additional sources of funding.

The Diversity Challenge

The plan encompassed many kinds of recovery activities, including both restoring and improving damaged and inadequate physical infrastructure and carrying out non–physical

---

[1] Financial Oversight and Management Board for Puerto Rico, *New Fiscal Plan for Puerto Rico: Restoring Growth and Prosperity*, San Juan, P.R.: Financial Oversight and Management Board for Puerto Rico, May 30, 2018, p. 12.

[2] Discounting is the appropriate procedure for measuring the true resource cost of any activity that extends over time. But as will be discussed later, the plan does not explicitly prescribe the timing of expenditures on COAs. This determination will have to be done in subsequent recovery plan implementation work. Without a representation of timing, discounting cannot be validly applied. The timing issue is discussed in detail below. In any case, if the timing of alternate plans is similar, the real discount rate low, and the horizon not very long, the two formulations are likely to give similar results in terms of comparing the costs of alternate plans.

infrastructure–related activities. The kinds of physical infrastructure that may need restoration or improvement include

- housing
- schools
- hospitals and medical clinics
- electrical generation, transmission, and distribution facilities
- water treatment and waste water plants
- roads, bridges, ports, and airports
- communications equipment and networks
- public buildings, including administrative, public safety, and museums
- natural resources, such as coral reefs and estuaries
- general economic—such as agricultural or tourist-related—infrastructure.

Within each of these categories of physical infrastructure, which essentially span the entire physical infrastructure of a modern industrial economy, a diverse set of restoration or improvement activities may be required by each COA, including

- simple rebuilding to predisaster condition
- rebuilding and improving to meet current regulations (such as those of the Environmental Protection Agency)
- rebuilding and improving to improve disaster resilience (which could include rebuilding in a different location)
- rebuilding and improving in other dimensions, such as using more appropriate fuels for power plants or upgrading electricity distribution and communications networks
- constructing new infrastructure for activities that improve Puerto Rico's future, such as industrial parks, business incubators, and research and development centers.

The additional kinds of recovery activities, beyond those related to physical infrastructure, include

- making incentive payments to individuals or businesses to induce specific kinds of behavior, such as subsidies for home insurance purchases
- making transfer payments to individuals or businesses to generally alleviate long-term hardships, such as grants for small business recovery, including agriculture
- organizing and staffing training programs to improve employment opportunities in Puerto Rico in general and to ensure that there is sufficient human capital to engage in recovery-related investments in particular
- improving emergency response planning and future execution, including organizing, hiring, and training response teams
- compiling information, such as inventories of public buildings and cultural resources
- hiring and training personnel to improve enforcement of regulations
- policy decisions, such as employment regulations, including minimum wage–type rules; business regulations, such as permit requirements; environmental regulations; and import and export laws.

These descriptions show that we were required to cost a remarkable diversity of activities—essentially everything a modern economy does. We attacked this problem using a diverse set of resources and SMEs, including our own HSOAC expertise; FEMA and other U.S. government personnel; cognizant Puerto Rican governmental and nongovernmental entities; and subcontractors we specifically engaged for this purpose. We also relied on federal resources (such as the U.S. Department of Transportation's Intelligent Transportation Systems Costs Database) and commercial cost estimation software and reference materials in consultation with the SMEs.

A Centralized or Decentralized Approach to Cost Analysis

The first decision we had to make was whether to have a centralized or decentralized approach to costing the COAs in our 12 recovery sectors. That is, should there be a central costing team responsible for all cost estimates, or should the estimates be done independently by—and the bulk of the costing resources given to—each sector team, with overall guidance and review provided by a small central team of expert cost analysts with broad-based experience. We opted for the second approach. This was based on the substantial number of COAs, their sectoral specificity, the technical complexity of infrastructure and other investments, and the great diversity of the activities included in the recovery plan. We judged that, based on these factors, any benefits from a centralized approach would be small when compared with the benefits from the in-depth specific sectoral knowledge a decentralized approach could bring to bear. Thus, sectors individually chose the cost estimation approach they judged most appropriate given the information available—subject to some basic common assumptions, such as time horizon and labor cost factors.

One common practice across all the sectors was that all the cost estimates were exposed to as wide a set of SMEs as possible for review and comment. Circulation specifically included cognizant persons in Puerto Rico, both in and out of government; FEMA personnel and others from the continental United States (CONUS) working on the ground in Puerto Rico; and all cognizant U.S. government agencies. All of this was in addition to HSOAC's formal quality assurance process for review, as well as the fact that a draft of the plan was released to the public (specifically, posted on the Puerto Rico governor's website) on July 9, 2018, for comments.[3]

Each sector team could approach each COA's cost in one of several ways:

- Build a bottom-up model of the COA, identifying the physical resources needed to carry it out, and estimating the cost of those resources.
- Use an existing model, or a set of cost-estimating relations, that is based on historical data on the cost of identical or analogous activities.

[3] Central Office of Recovery, Reconstruction, and Resiliency, "Transformation and Innovation in the Wake of Devastation: An Economic and Disaster Recovery Plan for Puerto Rico," San Juan, P.R.: Central Office of Recovery, Reconstruction, and Resiliency, July 9, 2018, preliminary draft manuscript.

- Use estimates provided by cognizant SMEs, including those from HSOAC, Puerto Rico private or public organizations, federal agencies, or subcontractors.

The individual sector volumes associated with this project give the relevant detail for how the specific COAs were costed.[4]

Costs Included and Not Included in the Plan

When we report the costs of recovery activities, we are only including costs for which *a specific payment must be made by some source* in order to carry out the COA. This can then be compared with available funding sources, which we discuss in Chapter 3. A funding source may include, for example, a federal government program. We are *not* including all the costs to society that may be associated with implementing these COAs but that do *not* have to be specifically reimbursed by some source in order for the COAs to be accomplished; rather, these costs are *imposed* on society in the course of carrying out the COA, and society must bear them. In general policy discussions these are sometimes referred to as unfunded mandates.[5] Examples of COAs that may impose some costs on society that we do not include would be the following:

- COAs that call for *better enforcement of regulations*, which may impose cost on individuals and businesses for compliance.
- COAs that call for *reorganization of economic activity in certain sectors*, which may lead to at least temporary job loss for some, with its associated economic hardship, and unemployment payments by the government of Puerto Rico.
- Any COA that involves changing a government policy, which can bring substantial costs in negotiating the details of the policy change, as well as costs in implementation, such as writing specific regulations. (There may also be political costs with such changes, including loss of goodwill among winning and losing factions. Even if a policy change is good for society as a whole, there will often be parts of society that suffer losses from the change. This political cost is nonmonetary.)

Just as we are not including any estimates of costs that are not reimbursed by some funding source, we are not including a monetary measure of the societal benefits that would be gained from carrying out the COA, such as improved health, safety, or income. Ideally, COAs would have comprehensive estimates of benefits—monetized or nonmonetized—that, when combined with cost information, including noncompensated societal costs, would make possible a straightforward cost-benefit assessment of each COA. Given the time and resource constraints of

---

[4] Links to the individual sector volumes can be found at RAND Corporation, undated.

[5] Of course, some entity may choose to compensate various groups for these imposed costs, but there is no need to do so in order to ensure that the COA is carried out. A convenient way to distinguish the two cost types is to ask, "If this cost is not paid, will the required resources for carrying out the COA be made available?" If the cost is hiring workers or purchasing goods and services from businesses, the costs clearly must be paid, and a funding source is required. If the costs are imposed, as in the examples in this section, no reimbursement is needed to ensure the COA is accomplished.

this project, and the complex nature of the benefits and nonreimbursed costs of many COAs, we were unable to carry out the analysis at this level. Instead, the sector teams, working in the iterative, expert- and stakeholder-driven process of COA identification and analysis, only chose COAs they judged would have positive net benefits. That is, each COA, if implemented, would provide societal benefits greater than its monetary and nonmonetary societal cost—again, based on a judgmental, expert-based, assessment.

We will illustrate next some of the methodologies, and then discuss some of the overall challenges of making these kinds of recovery cost estimates.

Examples of Cost Estimation Approaches

Personnel-Only Courses of Action

We begin with a simple example of *bottom-up models* of COAs. The only physical resources needed to carry out some COAs were personnel, and so the only costs were personnel costs. Here we define personnel costs as fully burdened labor rates, including salary, fringe benefits, and an indirect cost factor for material, energy, and purchased services associated with employment; this represents office accommodation, information technology support, administrative support, and the like. Examples of COAs with only personnel costs include

- training programs
- emergency response planning, including organizing response and recovery teams
- compiling information, such as inventories of public inventories and cultural resources
- community outreach programs
- enforcement of regulations.

Of course, to the extent that personnel have to be trained to perform these functions, the cost of the trainers must also be included. Such costs could be upfront or recurring. For example, in training programs there would be the upfront costs of the hiring and initial training of the trainers, and the recurring costs of their continued employment.

For these kinds of COAs the sector teams defined the COA in terms of the number of personnel needed, and for how many years, to carry them out. To the extent that the team size may vary over time, or that some workers might be part-time, we adjusted all personnel levels to full-time equivalents. All sectors then applied a common *cost per worker* factor to the full-time equivalent level to ensure that the COAs in the various sectors are treated uniformly.

Cost-per-Worker Factors

For an average worker in Puerto Rico, we use a standard annual labor cost of $62,300. This is the average *fully burdened* cost of a government employee in Puerto Rico, including associated material, energy, and purchased services costs. This figure is based on the 2016 total compensation per employee in the Puerto Rican governmental sector, which is $38,700.[6] U.S. total compensation of employees is 147 percent of wages and salaries, which implies a base salary of $26,400. In addition, U.S. spending on employment-related energy, materials, and purchased services is 52 percent of total compensation of employees in the "General Government" sector (the closest available analogue).[7] Applying this factor to total compensation gives a fully burdened personnel cost of $58,800 in 2016 dollars. This is equivalent to $62,300 in 2018 dollars, after inflating by the 6 percent growth of nominal gross domestic product (GDP) per worker between 2016 and 2018.

For projects requiring personnel with unique expertise in a technical field, such as architects, engineers, or other SMEs, we use a standard annual labor cost of $124,600 for Puerto Rico residents, which is double the average government rate. This judgmental factor of two was based on discussions with government budgeting experts in Puerto Rico. It is also supported by U.S. Bureau of Labor Statistics data. The annual mean wage for architects and engineers in Puerto Rico is $55,500.[8] Adjusting this base salary by the total compensation and overhead factors described above yields a total labor cost of $123,700.

For a CONUS-based contractor, we use a standard annual labor cost of $227,300. This is based on the median base salary of $98,000 for an electrical engineer from Bureau of Labor Statistics data,[9] adjusted to a fully burdened cost using the ratios mentioned above, plus estimated travel expenses of approximately $10,000 (assuming four trips of four to five days to Puerto Rico).

If a COA requires specialized CONUS-based experts, with long-term placement in Puerto Rico, we use a judgmental estimate of $10,000 per week based on discussions with contractors currently in Puerto Rico.

We also anticipated that the private sector will participate in task force meetings or related activities in carrying out several COAs. However, based on evidence from public-private partnerships (P3s), we estimated that it will do so voluntarily and will not be compensated.

---

[6] Government of Puerto Rico, Office of the Governor, Planning Board, *Apéndice Estadístico/Statistical Appendix*, San Juan, P.R.: Government of Puerto Rico, 2016, Tables 11 and 33.

[7] U.S. Bureau of Economic Analysis, "Industry Data," web database, undated.

[8] U.S. Bureau of Labor Statistics, "May 2017 State Occupational Employment and Wage Estimates: Puerto Rico," web database, last modified March 30, 2018a.

[9] The base salary estimate for a CONUS-based engineer (consultant) is based on the median salary for an electrical engineer derived from U.S. Bureau of Labor Statistics, *Occupational Outlook Handbook*, 2018–2019 ed., Lanham, Md.: Bernan Press, 2018b. This choice was based on the need for repair, design, and development of communications, power generation, and other electrical and electronic equipment. To ensure consistency across COAs—so that cost differences were not entirely driven by different labor cost assumptions for similar professions—we used this cost figure for technical experts, unless there was a compelling reason to use a different labor rate.

An Example of a Personnel-Only COA

One example of a personnel-only education COA is "a multisector analysis to support resource allocation decisions related to schools" that will identify where to invest in school infrastructure, where to reassign teachers, where to invest in school-to-work programs, and other related decisions. This COA is referred to as EDU 4 in the recovery plan.[10] We define this as five full-time equivalent SMEs drawn from Puerto Rico universities and three full-time equivalent outside consultants (for particularly specialized work). Based on the factors laid out above, this has an estimated cost of 5 × $124,600 + 3 × $520,000 = $2.2 million. In this estimate we assume that other stakeholder groups would not be compensated for participation in discussions related to this COA. We note the cost could be lower if some or all of the faculty time is covered by the universities.

Courses of Action with a Relatively Simple Bottom-Up Structure

A bottom-up model for some COAs will be relatively simple, consisting of one measure of number of activities undertaken and one measure of cost per activity. One set of examples would be incentive payments to individuals to change their behavior, or transfer payments to individuals and businesses to generally alleviate hardship. For this approach, the COA would have to define the expected number of recipients, and the expected cost per recipient. It may also be useful to distinguish classes of recipients, such as agricultural versus touristic versus other kinds of businesses. While these COAs may have a "simple" structure for estimation, a great deal of analysis (or judgment) may be required to accurately estimate both number of recipients and cost per recipient.

Construction and Repair COAs

At the opposite end of the complexity spectrum from personnel-only COAs are the (many) construction and repair COAs, also referred to as restoring and improving damaged and inadequate physical infrastructure. The construction and repair costs incurred to bring the physical structure or facility to the required level are upfront costs; costs that would be incurred on an annual basis to operate and maintain the structure or facility are recurring costs. For rebuilt infrastructure, we only included recurring, or O&M, costs that would be *above and beyond* the level typically incurred before the disaster—which, because of Puerto Rico's broader financial challenges,[11] was often too low for effective operation. Thus, facility O&M costs that were being paid prior to the hurricanes, and that would resume at previous levels once the facility was repaired, were not included. However, if O&M costs were to increase because structural improvements and technological upgrades made to the structure also inherently increased

---

[10] Government of Puerto Rico, 2018, p. 309.

[11] More information concerning predisaster economic conditions, as well as the effects of the hurricanes, can be found at RAND Corporation, undated.

required O&M, or simply because O&M expended before the disaster was too low for effective operation, then these incremental O&M costs were included in the cost of the COA.[12]

Thus, for example, if a given structure or facility was simply repaired to its previous state, and if the O&M incurred before the disaster was adequate for effectively operating and maintaining it after the repair, then the repair cost would be an upfront cost, and the recurring cost would be zero. On the other hand, for new infrastructure, all O&M costs would be *above and beyond* and are included in the cost of the COA.

Given the complexity of construction and repair work, the ideal cost estimates would be based on expert planning, facility class by facility class, from organizations that actually plan or carry out such projects in Puerto Rico. This is especially important because many of these facilities have unique size- or location-related aspects that affect costs. Ideally, the cost estimate would be based on a complete physical description of the activity, including number of persons employed for planning or administrative activities and the square footage and bill of materials for rebuilding, repair, and hazard mitigation activities. The availability of such in-depth, expert planning estimates varies by sectors, and in the immediate aftermath of the disaster, many persons who would be qualified to do such estimates were concerned with other urgent short-term tasks such as cleanup and safety-related measures.

One alternate approach, with less fidelity, would be to rely on average planning factors from publicly available or commercial cost-estimating resources. Potential sources include the RSMeans construction cost database,[13] the *Craftsman 2018 National Building Cost Manual*,[14] and the CostLab software from CBRE Business Analytics (formerly Whitestone Research Corporation).[15] Various websites from professional associations, and academic reports and papers, also contain such cost-factor data. Expert judgment can also be used as a source of such planning factors.

For example, for several Communications and Information Technology Sector COAs, we relied on cost factors relevant to implementing state-of-the art, survivable, resilient communications infrastructure. Specifically, we estimate the costs of trenching and installing conduit across the island, through which government entities or private companies could lay buried fiber optic cable. We use common unit costs for trenching of $10 per linear foot in flat terrain and $270 per linear foot in mountainous terrain, as well as common cost factors for

---

[12] This approach was recommended by the FEMA sponsor of this work, who wanted to ensure that recovery investments would support increased resilience in the future.

[13] See RSMeans, homepage, undated.

[14] Ben Moselle, ed., *Craftsman 2018 National Building Cost Manual*, Carlsbad, Calif.: Craftsman Book Company, 2017.

[15] See CBRE Business Analytics, "CostLab," webpage, undated. For this project we relied on earlier print references, including Douglas Abate, Michael Towers, Richard Dotz, Luca Romani, and Peter S. Lufkin, *The Whitestone Facility Maintenance and Repair Cost Reference 2009–2010*, Santa Barbara, Calif.: Whitestone Research, 2009.

conduit, handholes, and facilities to house signal regeneration equipment.[16] Thus, costs reflect the unique topography and challenges of construction in Puerto Rico. Similarly, for the Public Buildings Sector, we estimate a standard new construction cost of $225 per square foot for certain classes of facilities.[17] Across several sectors, including Public Buildings and Transportation, we used facility-specific O&M cost factors from common industry reference guides.

Another approach would be judgment-based estimates from knowledgeable sources. In this case, an analogy approach is generally viewed as preferable in the cost-estimating community—that is, one finds the best analogue for the COA in terms of activities undertaken elsewhere, and that can be used as the cost estimate, perhaps with judgmental adjustment for size of activity or location-specific factors. Potential analogues would be activities undertaken for recovery from Hurricanes Katrina or Sandy, along with previous U.S.-based projects to improve infrastructure, housing, and community resilience. For specific infrastructure projects, one can also draw on cost studies of similar federal and state programs.

For both the average planning factor approach and the analogy approach, one must take into account any factors unique to Puerto Rico. Construction costs are generally expected to be lower in Puerto Rico than in CONUS; for example, the *Craftsman 2018 National Building Cost Manual* notes that Puerto Rico costs are 21 percent below the average.[18] However, any recovery-related surge in demand for construction would tend to increase costs. Based on discussions with knowledgeable persons, we assessed that these factors would be of similar magnitude and—in the absence of any other specific estimate—offset one another.[19] The appendix to this chapter discusses how the surge issue might be dealt with more formally—which our time and resource constraints did not allow.

Courses of Action That Do Not Require Funding

Some COAs have no direct costs that require recovery funding support. These are generally COAs that involve policy changes, such as employment regulations, including minimum wage–type rules; business regulations, such as permit requirements; environmental regulations, which

---

[16] This is based on unit costs in Cambridge Systematics, *Rural Interstate Corridor Communications Study: Report to States*, Washington, D.C.: Federal Highway Administration, February 2009.

[17] This is based on analysis of several classes of public building (e.g., schools, hospitals, police stations) using the RSMeans software, including adjustments for Puerto Rico–specific cost factors.

[18] Moselle, 2017, p. 8.

[19] Construction industry experts estimate that offsetting factors, including the temporary surge in demand for construction equipment and materials (as well as transportation), would generally be of a similar order of magnitude as island-specific construction cost factors, but in the opposite direction. For example, the *Engineering News-Record* surveyed construction industry economists and analysts after Hurricane Katrina who estimated that regional construction costs would increase by 10 to 20 percent in the short term (6 to 24 months) following the storm; see T. Grogan and W. J. Angelo, "Katrina Gives Inflation a Second Wind," *ENR Cost Report*, 3Q, 2005, pp. 66–68. However, construction experts indicated that cost factors for Puerto Rico were less likely to reflect surge costs than the general high cost of goods in Puerto Rico, which reflect relatively higher taxes and fuel prices.

can affect businesses and individuals (such as car smog-device inspections); and import and export laws. These kinds of COAs may in general have other costs to society, which are not reimbursed by any funding source, as well as political costs, as illustrated in the section "Costs Included and Not Included in the Plan." If implementing such policy changes would require hiring additional staff, specifically paid for by a recovery-funding source, those employment costs were counted.

Estimated Costs for Puerto Rico's Recovery

The portfolios selected by the government of Puerto Rico—addressing the full set of comprehensive capital investments and strategic initiatives—comprise the recovery activities included in Puerto Rico's recovery plan and provide the basis for total cost estimates for the plan.[20] The recovery plan includes 276 individual COAs across the 12 recovery sectors. The total estimated cost of these recovery actions in 2018 dollars is $139 billion, which includes $105 billion in upfront costs and $34 billion in recurring costs incurred over the 11-year period 2018–2028. For context, the $105 billion in upfront cost is similar to Puerto Rico's annual GDP. Table 2.1 shows the cost of the plan disaggregated by sector, and by upfront versus recurring cost. It shows that costs are primarily driven by Housing ($33 billion), Water ($30 billion), and Energy ($26 billion), followed by Education ($15 billion)—these four sectors account for nearly 75 percent of the total cost of the plan.

[20] Capital investments and strategic initiatives are described in Chapter 1.

Table 2.1. Cost of Recovery Plan by Sector, 2018–2028, and by Upfront Versus Recurring Cost (in millions of 2018 dollars)

Sector	Total Cost	Upfront Cost	Recurring Cost	Number of COAs
Communications and Information Technology	3,190	1,860	1,330	33
Community Planning and Capacity Building	600	60	530	15
Economics	6,330	6,140	190	40
Education	15,230	7,720	7,520	13
Energy	26,000	15,000	11,000	27
Health and Social Services	6,340	5,320	1,020	31
Housing	32,560	30,050	2,510	12
Municipalities	160	30	130	11
Natural and Cultural Resources	3,870	3,520	350	30
Public Buildings	5,840	5,090	750	12
Transportation	8,440	6,310	2,130	22
Water	29,980	23,540	6,440	30
TOTAL	138,540	104,650	33,890	276

Figure 2.1 presents a disaggregation of costs within certain sectors. Each of these categories—unique to each sector—is a collection of some of the COAs in the sector, and each COA is included in one and only one category. This disaggregation illustrates the sectoral specificity, technical complexity, and diversity of activities in the recovery plan. For example, in the Housing Sector ($33 billion in total costs), repairing and reducing the vulnerability of housing stock accounts for the majority of costs ($27 billion), followed by stabilizing the housing market ($4.7 billion) and improving housing market infrastructure ($0.9 billion). More detail for each of the sectors, including specific recovery activities and itemized costs for individual COAs, can be found in the individual sector volumes written by HSOAC that are associated with this project.[21]

[21] Links to these can be found at RAND Corporation, undated.

Figure 2.1. Cost Disaggregation for Selected Sectors (in millions of 2018 dollars)

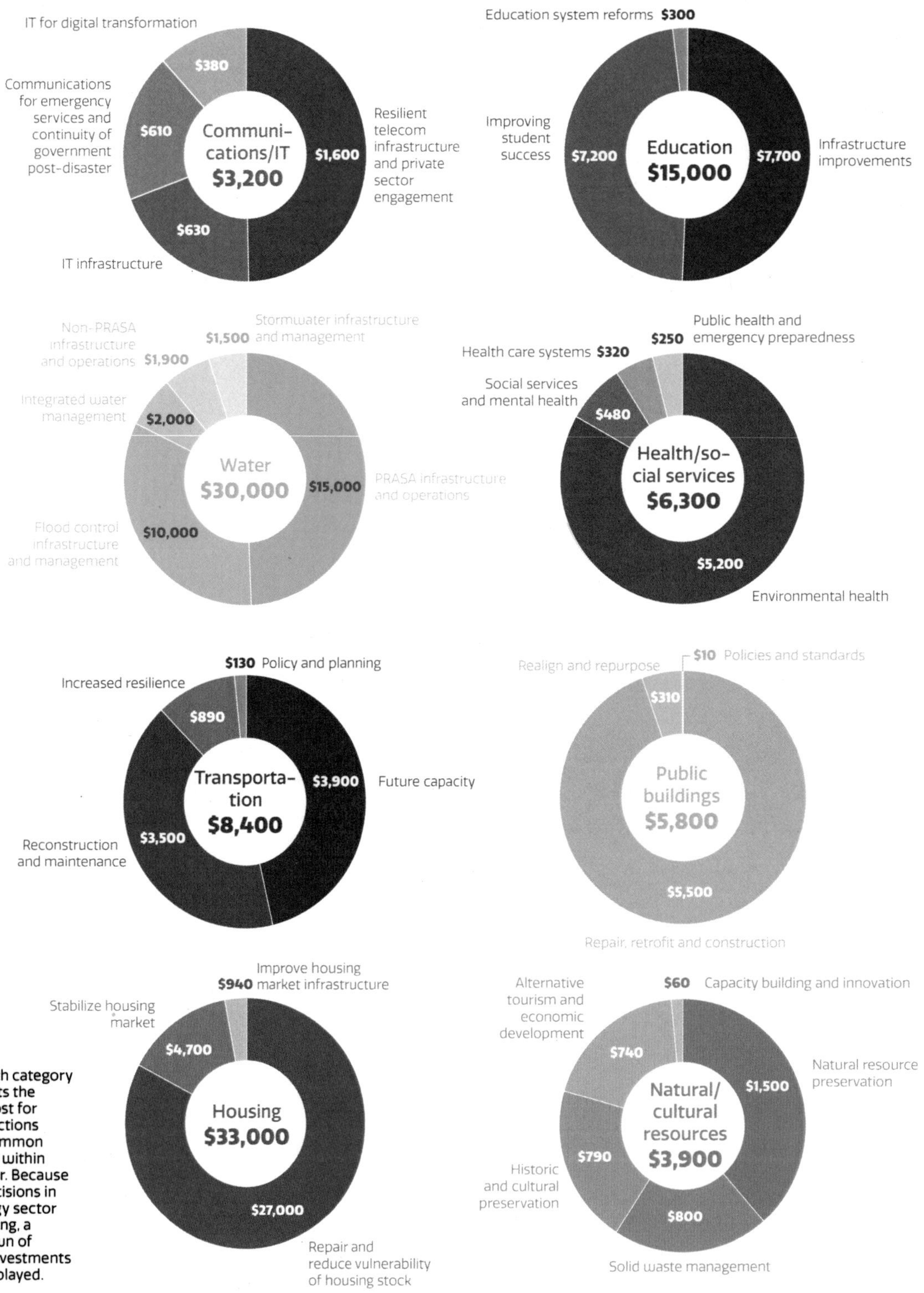

Note: Each category represents the overall cost for a set of actions with a common objective within the sector. Because many decisions in the energy sector are ongoing, a breakdown of energy investments is not displayed.

SOURCE: Government of Puerto Rico, 2018, p. 160.

Chapter Summary

This chapter has described the methodology for estimating the cost of Puerto Rico's recovery plan; cost estimates were made for each COA included in the plan. We laid out a key set of ground rules for cost estimation, whose goal was to ensure consistency of the cost estimates. COA-specific cost estimates, developed using a standard set of rules, and cross-COA comparisons can directly support prioritization of resources. The primary challenge of the cost analysis was the sheer number and diversity of the activities included in the plan—essentially everything a modern economy involves.

We used a decentralized approach to cost estimation, whereby sectors individually chose the cost estimation approach they judged most appropriate given the information available—subject to the ground rules mentioned above. This choice was based on the substantial number of COAs, their sectoral specificity, the technical complexity of infrastructure and other investments, and the great diversity of the activities included in the recovery plan. We judged that, based on these factors, any benefits from a centralized approach would be small compared with the benefits from the in-depth specific sectoral knowledge a decentralized approach could bring to bear.

One common practice across all the sectors was that all the cost estimates were exposed to as wide a set of SMEs as possible, for review and comment. Circulation specifically included cognizant persons in Puerto Rico, both in and out of government; FEMA personnel and other CONUS-based persons working on the ground in Puerto Rico; and all cognizant U.S. government agencies. All of this was in addition to HSOAC's formal quality assurance process for review and posting an early draft of the recovery plan online for public comment.

Puerto Rico's recovery plan, submitted by the governor of Puerto Rico to Congress on August 8, 2018, includes 276 individual COAs across the 12 sectors. The total estimated cost of these COAs is $139 billion, which includes $105 billion in upfront costs and $34 billion in recurring costs. The largest sectors of the recovery plan in terms of costs include Housing ($33 billion), Water ($30 billion), Energy ($26 billion), and Education ($15 billion); these four sectors account for nearly 75 percent of the total cost of the plan.

Appendix to Chapter 2: A More Formal Approach to Cost Analysis

This appendix presents a formal description of the costs of implementing a recovery plan. It illustrates many of the complexities that may be involved in determining the costs of the plan; in practical terms, cost estimates may have to be done in a simpler way because data, or time and resources, do not exist to support estimation in the detail presented here. We believe it is useful to keep this more complete framework in mind when making decisions on what can actually be done given any set of constraints. We have illustrated throughout how we simplified this more complete framework in our work on Puerto Rico's recovery plan.

Definitions

Before turning specifically to cost, we begin with a formal characterization of any recovery plan: A *recovery plan* is a set of *NR* COAs. We define the variable r $(r = 1, \ldots, NR)$ as an index over the COAs. For reference, a complete table of all the variables and their definitions is included as Table 2.2 at the end of this appendix. As has been noted, Puerto Rico's recovery plan comprises 276 COAs.

Here we note that COAs may be divisible or not. Some COAs are binary—that is, they are either implemented or they are not. (An example of this would be in the Communications and Information Technology Sector: CIT 27, "Study Feasibility of Digital Identity."[22] That study is either done, at a cost of $2 million, or it is not, at a cost of zero.) But others are continuous—that is, they can be carried out at different levels. The costs included in the recovery plan are for carrying out each COA at the level of implementation deemed appropriate for fully achieving Puerto Rico's recovery. However, they could in theory be carried out at a lower level, with an associated lower cost. (An example of this would be in the Housing Sector: HOU 2, "Assess, Repair, and Mitigate Damaged Subsidized Rental Housing."[23] One could carry this out for all the damaged subsidized-rental housing, at a cost of $1 billion. One could also carry it out for only part of the damaged housing, at a lower cost. In the extreme one could "carry it out" at a level of zero—that is, not do it at all—at a cost of zero.)

We define the variable $R(r)$ $(r = 1, \ldots, NR)$ as the level at which each individual COA is implemented. In the case of binary COAs, $R(r)$ equals one or zero—the activity is either done

[22] CIT 27 is so defined: "Study existing models and public acceptance of a secure digital identity including its reliance on resilient power and communications to facilitate government and private-sector transactions." Its potential benefits are identified as "Helps enable secure digital transactions, reduce costs associated with validation and access to government services when privately held records are unavailable, and reduce potential for fraud and identity theft." Government of Puerto Rico, 2018, p. 238.

[23] HOU 2 is so defined: "Assess damage and resiliency improvement needs for public housing and privately owned rental housing that receives government subsidies. Rehabilitate and/or modernize subsidized rental housing to accommodate people with or without disabilities, including people with access and functional needs, seniors, veterans, the homeless, and others." Its potential benefits are identified as "Provides safe, secure housing for low-income and homeless persons. Repairs damaged properties. Provides energy conservation upgrades. Mitigates damage from future disaster events." Government of Puerto Rico, 2018, p. 287.

or it is not. In the case of continuous COAs, $R(r)$ can take any value between zero and one inclusive, representing the fraction of the full activity that is carried out. Again, in this case, the "full activity" is the level of implementation defined in the recovery plan.

At a high level of abstraction, we can represent the cost of carrying out the NR COAs at arbitrary levels as $TT\{R(1), R(2), \dots, R(NR)\}$, where TT is the total cost. $TT\{1, 1, \dots, 1\}$ would then be the cost of carrying out the plan if every COA were to be implemented at its maximum level.

A Relatively Simple Representation of Cost

We begin with an important simplifying assumption: The cost of carrying out any COA, at any level, is independent of the levels at which the other COAs are carried out. We introduce NR new functions, $T(r, R(r))$, each of which represents the cost of carrying out COA r at level $R(r)$. These are, of course, only meaningful if the cost of carrying out any COA is indeed independent of the levels at which the others are carried out. Then we characterize the function TT as

$$TT\{R(1), R(2), \dots, R(NR)\} = \sum_{r=1}^{NR} T(r, R(r)). \tag{2.1}$$

This says that the total cost of the plan is simply the sum of the costs of each of the NR COAs, with no cost-related interaction among them.

It is sometimes convenient to do analysis under the assumption that each COA is carried out at its maximum level—that is, that $R(r) = 1$ for all r. To facilitate that, we define a new function

$$C(r) = T(r, 1), \tag{2.2}$$

where $C(r)$ is the cost of carrying out COA r at its maximum level. We define the variable TC, the total cost of carrying out the entire recovery plan at its maximum level, as

$$TC = \sum_{r=1}^{NR} C(r) = TT\{1, 1, \dots, 1\}. \tag{2.3}$$

The cost analysis done for the recovery plan was carried out in this framework, in which the cost of doing one COA is independent of the level at which the others are carried out. We discuss in the section "How to Improve the Modeling of Cost," below, how this approach could be extended to more accurately reflect reality by incorporating cost-related interactions among the COAs. We were unable to perform this extension in the recovery plan cost analysis, as our time constraints could not accommodate the added scope of analysis required.

We next discuss how the timing of upfront and recurring costs is represented in the analysis.

The Nexus Between the Time Required to Incur All Upfront Costs and the Level of Recurring Costs

The body of this chapter has discussed the distinction between upfront and recurring costs associated with each COA. Upfront costs are incurred only once, while recurring costs are incurred annually. For many COAs, it will be the case that recurring costs do not begin until after at least some of the work associated with the upfront costs has been completed.

For concreteness in this discussion, we will use a specific notional COA; this COA includes 100 units of total upfront costs to construct a facility. Once the facility has been built and is fully in operation, five units in recurring costs will be incurred per year—but there will be no recurring costs before the facility is fully in operation. Then the total cost of the COA depends on how long it takes to complete the construction. Let the time period of the recovery plan be NT years, indexed by the variable t ($t = 1, \ldots, NT$). Let the construction time for the upfront costs of the COA be $NC(r)$. Construction begins in year 1. Full operation will commence in year $NC(r) + 1$. If $NT = NC(r)$, total cost will be upfront cost (100) only, since the facility will not be operated within the time period of the plan. If $NT < NC(r)$, total cost will be $[100 + 5 * (NT - NC(r)]$. The facility will be operated for $[NT - NC(r)]$ years within the time period of the plan. If $NT > NC(r)$, only a fraction of the construction costs will be incurred during the plan time period.

An alternate formulation would allow partial operation of the facility after part of it had been constructed. There are many possible ways to represent this. One possible way—which we used as a default case in the recovery plan—is the following: In any year $t \leq NC(r)$ the facility is operating at a level proportional to the level of overall project completion in that year. Recurring cost in that year is (the level of operation) times (the annual recurring cost at full facility operation). Construction begins in year 1, and the project is completed uniformly across the $NC(r)$ years, so the level of overall project completion in any year t is $[t \,/\, NC(r)]$, and recurring cost in that year is $5 * [t \,/\, NC(r)]$. If $NC(r) < NT$, total recurring cost is[24]

$$\begin{aligned} &5 * [1/\,NC(r) + 2/\,NC(r) + \cdots + (NC(r) - 1)/\,NC(r) + \\ &\quad NC(r)/\,NC(r) + (NT - NC(r))] \\ &= 5 * [(NC(r) + 1)/2 + (NT - NC(r))] \\ &= 5 * [NT + 1/2 - NC(r)/2]. \qquad (2.4) \end{aligned}$$

There could be many patterns of how recurring costs vary with the completion of upfront costs, but whatever they may be, *the total level of recurring costs over the horizon of the plan will vary with the pattern of how upfront costs are incurred.* There may, of course, be some COAs for which the recurring costs are independent of when upfront costs are incurred, but we expect that most recurring costs will indeed vary with upfront cost timing, as in the examples in

[24] This is derived from $(1 + 2 + \ldots + n) = n * (n + 1)/2$. In mathematics lore, Carl Friedrich Gauss discovered this formula as a schoolboy. See NRICH Team, "Clever Carl," NRICH, webpage, last updated September 2012.

this section: Upfront costs are construction costs for a facility; recurring costs are the operating costs of the facility; and the level of operating cost depends on how much of the total construction work has been completed.

This is especially important for recovery programs such as Puerto Rico's because they generally require a very large amount of upfront investment costs—on the order of annual GDP in this case. Thus, we would expect these costs to be spread out considerably over time, especially compared with what construction times would be in a non-disaster-recovery environment, when total investment costs tend to be on the order of 15 to 20 percent of GDP.[25] The absorptive capacity of the economy—limitations in labor pools and the ability to produce or import construction equipment and materials—will constrain the level at which construction can occur in any given year. Thus, construction projects will likely take longer to complete than would have been the case in the absence of the disaster.

In the discussion above we explicitly posited that each COA's upfront costs will begin to be incurred in the first year of the recovery plan. The lack of absorptive capacity may lead to a delay in initiating some projects to a later year; this will also affect the level of recurring costs incurred over the plan.[26]

The recovery plan included all the upfront costs of the COAs, thus implicitly assuming that they could be completed before the end of the plan's time horizon. In calculating recurring costs, it is also implicitly assumed that all COAs are initiated in the first year of the recovery plan. A time period to complete upfront costs was estimated for each COA. In the absence of other information, the total level of recurring costs over the plan time period was estimated as follows: The recurring cost of each COA was defined in terms of dollars per year, say $\$X$, and this represented annual costs once the facility had been built and was fully in operation. Total recurring costs were estimated under the *facility operates at a level proportional to overall project completion* assumption, so that total recurring costs were $\$X * [NT + 1/2 - NC(r)/2]$. Thus, to the extent that absorptive capacity constraints might cause COA initiation to be delayed, or the time period to complete upfront costs to increase, total recurring costs will be overestimated. Also, to the extent that either delays in COA initiation or increases in the time period to complete result in upfront costs extending *beyond* the time horizon of the recovery plan, upfront costs *within* the recovery plan time period will be overestimated.

---

[25] The ratio of gross domestic investment to GDP in Puerto Rico has averaged 18 percent between 2007 and 2016, though only 15 percent in the crisis period between 2014 and 2016. See Government of Puerto Rico, Office of the Governor, Planning Board, 2016, Table 1. If we make an adjustment for government funded investment, based on the ratio between government and private investment in the United States in 2017 (19 percent), the figures rise to 21 percent between 2007 and 2016, and 17 percent in the crisis period between 2014 to 2016. For U.S. data, see U.S. Bureau of Economic Analysis, "Gross Domestic Product, Third Quarter 2018 (Third Estimate); Corporate Profits, Third Quarter 2018 (Revised Estimate)," Washington, D.C., December 21, 2018, Table 3.

[26] For a discussion of absorptive capacity constraints in Puerto Rico, particularly as they relate to workforce issues, see RAND Corporation, 2019; see also RAND Corporation, undated.

How to Improve the Modeling of Cost

We return now to the general assumption that the cost of carrying out any COA, at any level, is independent of the levels at which the other COAs are carried out. This assumption was embodied in Equation (2.3):

$$TC = \sum_{r=1}^{NR} C(r) = TT\{1, 1, \dots, 1\}. \tag{2.3}$$

There are several ways in which this assumption can be violated in reality. For example, say that putting both communications and power lines underground are potential COAs. Doing both may cost less than twice the cost of doing one if the benefits of joint trenching and related activities can be shared. A relatively complex cost function would then result, in which the cost of some *set* of activities would depend on the level of *each* of the activities. Specifically, in this case the cost of doing any one COA in the set will be lower, the higher the level at which the others are carried out. Formally, the second cross partial derivatives of TC with respect to the $R(r)$ will be negative, and not zero as the linear formulation implies.

In the other direction, say the scale of doing all the COAs is such that the costs of labor or other inputs will be driven up; this is essentially the absorptive capacity phenomenon just discussed. Doing fewer than all may not lead to so large an input cost increase, so lowering the level at which some COAs are done may lower the cost of doing others. That is, the cost of any given level of a COA's upfront activity will itself depend on how much upfront activity is occurring in other COAs, and the cost of any given level of a COA's recurring activity will likewise depend on how much recurring activity is occurring in other COAs. Specifically, in this case the cost of doing any one COA will be higher, the higher the level at which the others are carried out. Formally, the second cross partial derivatives of TC with respect to the $R(r)$ will be positive, and not zero, as the linear formulation implies.

Incorporation of all these considerations into the recovery plan analysis was, as has been noted, infeasible due to time constraints. Further research into how to address them would have high value for future disaster recovery work. Among other things, a time dimension would have to be introduced into the equations that relate the level of COA activity to cost. In the next section we present one approach to doing this.

Formal Integration of the Absorptive Capacity Considerations

Here we will present one formal approach to addressing absorptive capacity considerations. We note, however, that this is a representative case only; there may well be other ways of incorporating absorptive capacity into cost analysis. The analyst will have to judge which is the most appropriate approach for whatever set of COAs are being considered. The approach we present here has the following structure.

COAs, as before, are indexed over r ($r = 1, \dots, NR$). Also, as before, the time period of the recovery plan is NT years, and the variable t ($t = 1, \dots, NT$) is an index of the years of the plan.

In considering the upfront cost of any COA, we make a distinction between the *physical work required* to carry out the COA and the *cost* of the COA. In the original formulation of cost (which is how it was approached in the recovery plan), if the upfront cost of a COA was $\$Y$, this was meant as the total cost of the project from start to finish. The unit costs of inputs to the project (of labor per hour, materials per ton, and so on) were assumed constant over the course of the project; these are BAU costs. Thus, when one-fourth of $\$Y$ was expended, one-fourth of the physical work was accomplished; when one-half of $\$Y$ was expended, one-half of the physical work was accomplished, and so on. As such, the proportion of the work accomplished after $Z\%$ of $\$Y$ has been expended, *at BAU prices*, is also $Z\%$. Here "the work" more precisely means the physical work required to carry out the COA. The distinction between physical work and cost is important when absorptive capacity constraints raise the unit costs of inputs to the project above BAU levels.

We now define the variables:

- $U(r,t)$ is the upfront cost of COA r incurred in time period t.
- $\Pi(r,t)$ is the proportion of the physical work required to carry out the upfront part of COA r that is accomplished in time t.
- $\Gamma(r)$ is the BAU cost of carrying out the entire upfront part of COA r. (This is the total upfront cost of COA r from the recovery plan.) Thus, if BAU costs prevail in all periods, the upfront cost in any period t will be $(\Gamma(r))(\Pi(r,t))$.
- $\alpha(t)$ is the "absorptive capacity acceleration factor" in period t. This is the ratio of unit input costs in period t to their BAU level. The same factor is assumed to apply to all input types in this representation. Thus, the upfront cost for COA r in period t is $U(r,t) = (\alpha(t))(\Gamma(r))(\Pi(r,t))$.

It remains to be specified how $\alpha(t)$ is determined. In this formulation we posit that it is an increasing function A of the total amount of upfront cost incurred in period t, valued at BAU prices. This is then an index of the volume of upfront COA activity, which is the underlying cause of the absorptive capacity–related pressure on input costs.

$$\alpha(t) = A\left(\sum_{r=1}^{NR} \Gamma(r)\,\Pi(r,t)\right). \tag{2.5}$$

Total upfront costs incurred over the horizon of the plan are then

$$\sum_{t=1}^{NT}\sum_{r=1}^{NR} U(r,t) = \sum_{t=1}^{NT}\sum_{r=1}^{NR} \alpha(t)\,\Gamma(r)\Pi(r,t). \tag{2.6}$$

We note that each $\Pi(r,t)$ enters Equation (2.6) twice: first, as explicitly shown in the equation, and second, as a determinant of $\alpha(t)$. The equation sums up how annual upfront costs are determined: The only *decision variables* are the $\Pi(r,t)$, which indicate how much work is accomplished on the upfront part of each COA in period t. These are then multiplied by the BAU cost factors, and further escalated by the absorptive-capacity-factor $\alpha(t)$; all of which—including the functional form of the function A that determines the $\alpha(t)$—are *parameters or other input factors*.

Above we discussed how recurring costs in any year would be related to the proportion of upfront work accomplished through that year. We can now formalize those relations by adding the following variables.

- $V(r,t)$ is the recurring cost of COA r incurred in time period t.
- $P(r,t)$ is the proportion of the physical work required to carry out the upfront part of COA r that is accomplished *through* time t (as opposed to *in* time t). This is defined as

$$P(r,t) = \sum_{\tau=1}^{t} \Pi(r,t). \tag{2.7}$$

- $K(r)$ is the annual recurring cost of COA r when all the work required for the upfront part has been completed. (This was referred to as $\$X$ above.)

Then $V(r,t) = K(r)\big(P(r,t)\big)$ is the formal expression for annual recurring costs consistent with the verbal characterization above, and total recurring costs over *NT* are

$$\sum_{t=1}^{NT}\sum_{r=1}^{NR} V(r,t) = \sum_{t=1}^{NT}\sum_{r=1}^{NR} K(r)P(r,t). \tag{2.8}$$

Finally, total costs associated with any pattern of COA implementation $\Pi(r,t)$ are

$$\sum_{t=1}^{NT}\sum_{r=1}^{NR}[\alpha(t)\Gamma(r)\Pi(r,t)] + \sum_{t=1}^{NT}\sum_{r=1}^{NR} K(r)P(r,t). \tag{2.9}$$

Equation (2.9) is the analogue, in the absorptive capacity case, of Equation (2.1) defining total cost (*TT*) in the "relatively simple" case with which we began this appendix.

Again, the only decision variables are the $\Pi(r,t)$, which indicate how much work is accomplished on the upfront part of each COA in period t. The $P(r,t)$ are a function of the $\Pi(r,t)$, and everything else in the equation is either a parameter or other input factor, such as the functional form of the function A that determines $\alpha(t)$.

In this formulation recurring costs are not affected by absorptive capacity factors; one could also incorporate such a relationship into the analysis. It would be parallel to the BAU cost versus the absorptive capacity–related escalation factor structure used to represent upfront costs.

All Variables

Table 2.2 presents all variables in this appendix.

Table 2.2. Names and Definitions of Variables

Name	Definition
NR	Number of COAs in the recovery plan (276, in this case).
$r\ (r = 1, \ldots, NR)$	An index over the COAs.
$R(r)\ (r = 1, \ldots, NR)$	The level at which each individual COA is implemented. $0 \leq R(r) \leq 1$.
$TT\{R(1), R(2), \ldots, R(NR)\}$	The total cost of carrying out the NR COAs at arbitrary implementation levels.
$T(r, R(r))$	The cost of carrying out COA r at level $R(r)$ (only meaningful if the cost of carrying out any COA is independent of the levels at which the others are carried out).
$C(r) = T(r, 1)$	The cost of carrying out COA r at its maximum level.
$TC = \sum_{r=1}^{NR} C(r)$	The total cost of carrying out the entire recovery plan at its maximum level.
NT	The time period of the recovery plan in years (11, in this case).
$t\ (t = 1, \ldots, NT)$	An index of the NT years of the recovery plan.
$NC(r)$	The construction time for the upfront costs of COA r in years.
$U(r, t)$	The upfront cost of COA r incurred in time period t.
$\Pi(r, t)$	The proportion of the physical work required to carry out the upfront part of COA r that is accomplished in time t.
$\Gamma(r)$	The BAU cost of carrying out the entire upfront part of COA r.
$\alpha(t)$	The absorptive capacity acceleration factor in period t. This is the ratio of unit input costs in period t to their BAU levels.
$V(r, t)$	Recurring cost of COA r incurred in time period t.
$P(r, t)$	The proportion of the physical work required to carry out the upfront part of COA r that is accomplished through time t (as opposed to in time t).
$K(r)$	Annual recurring cost of COA r when all the work required for the upfront part has been completed.

Appendix Summary

This appendix has presented a formal description of the costs of implementing a recovery plan, and illustrates many of the complexities that may be involved in determining the costs of such a plan. In practical terms, cost estimates may have to be done in a simpler way because data, or time and resources, do not exist to support estimation in the detail presented here. We believe it is useful to keep this more complete framework in mind when making decisions on what can actually be done given any set of constraints. We have illustrated throughout how what we did for Puerto Rico's recovery plan simplified from this more complete framework.

3. Funding Analysis

This chapter identifies potential funders and discusses a framework for allocating funding sources to individual COAs in Puerto Rico's recovery plan. Potential funding sources include federal governmental sources and nongovernmental sources, such as private-sector funding and philanthropic actors. Additional funding contributions will come from Puerto Rican governmental entities, at either the commonwealth or municipal level, and proceeds from revenue-generating projects. Some funders, particularly certain federal programs, will fund only a percentage of any project and require a matching contribution. As such, many COAs will necessarily have more than one funder.

Introduction to Funding Analysis

A funding plan is an allocation of funding sources to individual COAs. As was discussed in Chapter 2, we associate a cost with each COA, which is the amount of money that has to be paid to some entity to ensure that the COA is carried out. Thus, for the upfront cost portion of a construction COA, the cost would be the payment that must be made to the construction company in order to have the construction project completed. If there is ongoing maintenance required to carry out the COA, its cost is the sum of the annual payments that must be made to the entity that operates the facility to ensure that required maintenance is indeed done—for labor, supplies, and the like. Again, we include only ongoing costs that are above and beyond the costs that were regularly incurred before the disaster.

If these costs are going to be met, someone has to meet them; that "someone" is a funder. Table 3.1 lists the types of funders considered in this report.

We note again that not all societal costs associated with COAs will have to be funded; some—for example, the cost of complying with new regulations—will be imposed on individuals and businesses, and no specific funding source is required. We also note that some funders, especially some U.S. government funders, will fund only a certain percentage of any project—generally in the 75–90 percent range. They require that another funding source be found for the remainder, which is referred to as a matching contribution. In these cases, a COA would necessarily have more than one funder.

Table 3.1. Potential Funding Sources for Puerto Rico's Recovery Plan

Funding Source	Description
Disaster Relief Fund (DRF) appropriations	The federal government's DRF, administered by FEMA
Non-DRF appropriations	Specific additional non-DRF appropriations made for disaster relief in U.S. legislation, such as the Community Development Block Grant—Disaster Recovery (CDBG-DR) program from the U.S. Department of Housing and Urban Development (HUD), and other programs
Other federal programs	Regular ongoing federal programs, which are funded through normal appropriations and program budgeting
Insurance	Proceeds from private insurance
Government of Puerto Rico	Contributions by Puerto Rican governmental entities, at either the commonwealth or municipal level
Revenue-generating projects	Proceeds from COAs that are themselves revenue-generating projects
Private sector funding	Traditional direct private investment, institutional investors, and public-private partnerships
Philanthropic actors	Charitable foundations, corporate foundations, and individual donors
Local and international nongovernmental organizations (NGOs)	Organizations with a charitable mission, independent of any government, that carry out projects on the ground to benefit the community or society as a whole

A complete funding plan would indicate what organizations will fund how much of the costs of each COA. We can most easily think of it as a *funding matrix*, in which the rows represent COAs, or parts of COAs, and the columns represent funding organizations. Each element of the matrix would be the amount of each COA or part of a COA that is paid for by each funding organization. The sum across each row would be total funding going toward the associated COA or part of a COA. The sum down each column would be the total funding from each funding organization. The total of all cells in the matrix would, of course, be the total cost of the recovery program that is funded.

The phrase "the rows represent COAs, or parts of COAs" begs certain questions: Should a row include all the costs in a COA, or should each COA's costs be disaggregated across a set of rows? If the latter, what should the disaggregation be? Costs could be broken into specific types of costs, as represented in Table 3.2.

Table 3.2. Potential Disaster Recovery Cost Categories

Cost Category
Construction (repair or rebuild)
Construction (hazard mitigation)
Personnel, including workforce training and development
Equipment and materials
Operations and Maintenance
Financial incentives
Transfer payments

Furthermore, a funding matrix would ideally include information about

- upfront versus recurring costs—this is likely to be important, since funding agencies may, by policy, only support one or the other
- the year in which costs are incurred
- costs borne by primary funder versus matching contribution requirement.

The phrase "the columns represent funding organizations" also leads to a question: Does the term *funding organization* mean a larger agency such as a U.S. government department or a charitable organization, or a specific program within such an agency or organization? These distinctions would dictate the relative size and complexity of a funding matrix. Notionally, this funding matrix is presented in Table 3.3.

Table 3.3. Example Funding Matrix (in notional dollar amounts)

COA	Cost Category	Start Date	Funder 1	Funder 2	Funder 3	Total Funding
COA 1	Part 1a	Year 1	50	25	0	75
	Part 1b	Year 1	50	75	0	125
	Part 2	Year 2	50	0	50	100
	Part 3	Year 3	50	0	100	150
	Subtotal		200	100	150	450
COA 2	Part 1	Year 1	0	200	0	200
	Part 2	Year 2	0	300	0	300
	Subtotal		0	500	0	500
Total			**200**	**600**	**150**	**950**

In the rest of this chapter we will consider various ways one might address funding analysis.

Approaches to Funding Analysis

We considered three levels of detail in doing funding analysis:

1. identifying potential funding sources and estimating, if possible, the dollar value of their total contribution to the Puerto Rico COAs
2. identifying potential funding sources for each COA
3. constructing a complete funding matrix: identifying specific funders for each COA.

We did carry out options 1 and 2, but we did not carry out option 3. We will discuss each of these in turn, including a discussion of why we did not carry out option 3.

Identifying Potential Funding Sources and Estimating, If Possible, the Dollar Value of Their Total Contribution to the Puerto Rico Courses of Action

We identified potential funding sources in Table 3.1. The first four categories, which include federal government sources and private insurance, are *sources with estimated funding*—that is, sources for which we judge it useful to estimate the dollar value of their contribution to Puerto Rico's recovery. Below we give the basis on which we make each estimate. The additional sources are ones for which we do not judge it useful to estimate the dollar value of their contribution to Puerto Rico's recovery. This is because we found no analytically defensible basis on which to make such an estimate, and thus any such estimate would have no value for recovery planning. We will also discuss these sources below.

We note that in the recovery plan three broad categories of potential funding were presented to meet the estimated $139 billion cost of the plan. These include

1. funding known to be available
2. funding for which the amount available is known but the amount that Puerto Rico will receive is uncertain
3. funding that will be sought out from additional sources; success in obtaining these funds is not guaranteed.

The federal government and private insurance funding sources were divided into the first two categories. After further work in this area, we have concluded that making the distinction between the first two categories is not particularly useful. All funding estimates are in fact on a spectrum of uncertainty, and much of what we identified as *funding known to be available* is in fact uncertain to some degree. Thus, we believe it is analytically best to drop this distinction. All funding estimates were generated by plan analysts from FEMA and HSOAC; they are based on information available through July 2018.

The U.S. Government's Disaster Relief Fund

FEMA administers the DRF, which serves the entire nation. Congress, which is responsible for ensuring that the DRF has adequate funding to meet current and anticipated needs, appropriated $50 billion to the DRF in the three disaster-related supplemental bills of late FY 2017 and early FY 2018 (Public Laws 115-56, 115-72, and 115-123). Funds from the DRF are awarded by FEMA on a project-by-project basis. Table 3.4 lists the types of FEMA grants available from the DRF.

For each of these programs, FEMA estimated the following resources to be available through the DRF for Puerto Rico:

- **IA.** FEMA estimates that $0.8 billion will be awarded to qualifying applicants in Puerto Rico. This estimate includes only housing assistance as a recovery funding source, not other needs assistance. In July 2018 FEMA provided a low, medium, and high projection of IA to plan analysts. The high estimate was FEMA's then-current projection of what IA awards would ultimately be. The medium estimate accounted for potential overestimation due to proof of ownership requirements and disallowing cost comparison from wood to concrete. The low estimate also accounted for potential overestimation due to other eligibility restrictions. We are using FEMA's then-current projection—that is, the high estimate—which FEMA recommended to us as its best estimate.

Table 3.4. FEMA Disaster Relief Fund Programs

Funding Source	Description	Funding for Puerto Rico, Estimated as of July 2008 (in billions of 2018 dollars)
Individual assistance (IA)	Provides immediate relief and assistance to individuals and households; the IA program includes the Crisis Counseling Assistance and Training Program; Disaster Case Management; Disaster Legal Services; Disaster Unemployment Assistance; the Individuals and Households Program; and Mass Care and Emergency Assistance	$0.8 (housing assistance only)
Public assistance (PA)	Provides funds for repairing, restoring, and replacing facilities damaged by a disaster; FEMA PA Emergency Work categories include debris removal (Category A) and emergency protective measures (Category B). FEMA PA Permanent Work categories include roads and bridges (Category C); water control facilities (Category D); buildings and equipment (Category E); utilities (Category F); and parks, recreational, and other facilities (Category G).	$37.4 (Category C–G only)
Hazard Mitigation Grant Program (HMGP)	Provides grants to reduce the hazard risk of damage, hardship, loss, or suffering from future disasters	$3.0

- **PA.** FEMA estimates that $37.4 billion will be awarded. This estimate includes only Permanent Work (Categories C–G) as a recovery funding source, not Emergency Work (Categories A–B). Section 406 hazard mitigation funds are part of PA. In July 2018, FEMA provided a low, medium, and high projection of PA to plan analysts. The low estimate was based on the current cost estimate for specific projects that were expected to be approved as of March 2018. The medium estimate projected more damage lists being completed by the applicants, and new categories of applicants, such as those applying for Section 406 mitigation. The high estimate accounted for hidden damage and eligibility decisions being overturned by appeal, such as waivers for critical infrastructure. We are using FEMA's high estimate, which FEMA recommended to us as its best estimate.
- **HMGP.** As of July 2018, FEMA estimates that $3.0 billion will be awarded.

Our total estimate of DRF funds that will be available for Puerto Rico's recovery plan is thus $41.2 billion.

Specific Additional Non-DRF Appropriations Made for Disaster Relief in U.S. Legislation

Congress made specific additional disaster relief appropriations, beyond contributions to the DRF, in the three disaster-related supplemental bills of late FY 2017 and early FY 2018 (Public Laws 115-56, 115-72, and 115-123). It appropriated $35.4 billion to the CDBG-DR program; these funds are administered by HUD. Of the $35.4 billion, $19.9 billion has been directed to Puerto Rico's recovery effort; the rest was largely for Hurricane Harvey recovery in the South.[1] CDBG-DR funding does not require recipients to provide a nonfederal matching contribution. In fact, once the funds have been awarded to a state or territory, they can be used as "nonfederal" matching contributions for other federal grants.

The three disaster-related recovery bills also included $35 billion of non-DRF, non-CDBG-DR appropriations to federal agencies for specific disaster relief activities. Not all of the funds will be available to support the recovery activities in Puerto Rico's recovery plan. First, some of the funds—about $4.5 billion, based on the congressional language—are dedicated to federal expenses (e.g., federal agencies repairing their own hurricane-damaged facilities). Second, Puerto Rico will compete for a share of the remaining $30.5 billion in disaster funding with other states affected by Hurricanes Harvey, Irma, and Maria; recent wildfires; and other disasters. The total that will be allocated to Puerto Rico has not yet been determined. Based on the distribution of CDBG-DR allocations, plan analysts estimate that Puerto Rico will receive $21.2 billion.[2]

Regular Ongoing Federal Programs That Are Funded Through Normal Appropriations and Program Budgeting

The funding in this category comes from steady-state federal programs, which are funded through normal appropriations and program budgeting. These are authorized, ongoing federal programs that existed before the disaster. Analysts for the recovery plan, in consultation with FEMA, project that Puerto Rico will receive $9.4 billion per year in steady-state federal grants. This is based on the 2010 value of $6.9 billion in federal grant aid, escalated to 2018 using the U.S. nominal GDP growth rate of 35.7 percent over that period.[3] Much of this amount will be

---

[1] Public Law 115-56 included $7.4 billion of CDBG-DR funds, of which $1.5 billion was subsequently allocated to Puerto Rico; see HUD, "HUD and Puerto Rico Ink $1.5 Billion Disaster Recovery Grant Agreement," Washington, D.C., September 20, 2018. Public Law 115-123 included $28.0 billion of CDBG-DR funds, of which $18.4 billion was subsequently allocated to Puerto Rico; see HUD, "HUD Awards $28 Billion in CDBG-DR Funds," Washington, D.C.: April 11, 2018.

[2] The funds allocated in these bills are very usefully summarized in two documents; see William L. Painter, *2017 Disaster Supplemental Appropriations: Overview*, Washington, D.C.: Congressional Research Service, January 25, 2018; and U.S. Senate Committee on Appropriations, *Supplemental Appropriations for Disaster Relief and Recovery*, Washington, D.C.: U.S. Senate Committee on Appropriations, undated.

[3] U.S. Census Bureau, *Federal Aid to States for Fiscal Year 2010*, Washington, D.C.: U.S. Government Printing Office, September 2011.

pass-through funds provided directly to individuals. However, some programs may allow funds to be redirected for recovery needs. Plan analysts project that 32 percent of the funds will allow redirection for recovery needs. This is based on the Estudios Técnicos Inc. finding that 32 percent of grant aid to Puerto Rico is competitively awarded.[4] Plan analysts judge that these funds have the flexibility to be partly redirected to recovery activities and estimate that 10 percent of those funds will be reprogrammed to recovery-related activities. Thus, plan analysts estimate that $300 million in funds will be redirected to meet recovery needs each year. Over the 11-year horizon of the analysis, $3.3 billion of such funds will be available to Puerto Rico.[5]

Proceeds from Private Insurance

Private insurance proceeds will be available to support some recovery activities, though there is uncertainty about what the ultimate level of private insurance claim reimbursements will be. The *New Fiscal Plan for Puerto Rico: Restoring Growth and Prosperity*, certified by the Financial Oversight and Management Board of Puerto Rico on May 30, 2018, projects that $8 billion will be available in insurance proceeds; there are a wide range of estimates of insurance proceeds beyond the board's $8 billion estimate. Discussions with personnel at the Office of the Commissioner of Insurance of Puerto Rico led to an estimated range of $12 billion–$15 billion, with many caveats that the true figure is unknowable at this time. The government of Puerto Rico's April 5, 2018, version of the *New Fiscal Plan for Puerto Rico* included a $15.8 billion estimate.[6] AIR Worldwide estimated a range of $27 billion to $43 billion.[7] As the author of the recovery plan, the government of Puerto Rico ultimately chose the most conservative, $8 billion, estimate. As just noted, other sources estimate that private insurance claims will exceed this amount; to the extent that these claims are paid, more of the cost of the recovery plan will be covered.

Table 3.5 summarizes the funding levels estimated for the sources; the total is $93.6 billion.

---

[4] Estudios Técnicos Inc., *Snapshot of Federal Assistance Programs FY 2010*, Commonwealth of Puerto Rico, Office of Management and Budget, December 2013, p. 6.

[5] As was described in Chapter 2, we use a time horizon of 11 years for aggregating total costs and estimating recovery resources available. This time horizon was chosen to align with that of the Financial Oversight and Management Board's estimate of recovery *resources* available; see Financial Oversight and Management Board for Puerto Rico, 2018.

[6] Government of Puerto Rico, *New Fiscal Plan for Puerto Rico*, San Juan, P.R.: Government of Puerto Rico, April 5, 2018, p. 24.

[7] AIR Worldwide, "AIR Updates Insured Loss Estimates for Hurricane Maria," Press Release, Boston, December 6, 2017, p. 1.

Table 3.5. Funding Sources, with Estimates of Funding Levels

Funding Source	Estimated Funding Amount (in billions of 2018 dollars)
DRF IA	0.8
DRF PA	37.4
DRF HMGP	3.0
Non-DRF appropriations: CDBG-DR	19.9
Non-DRF appropriations: other	21.2
Regular federal programs	3.3
Private insurance	8.0
TOTAL	**93.6**

The Matching Contribution Issue

Several of the federal funding sources have a matching contribution requirement—that is, a percentage share of the total cost must be provided from another source. Table 3.6 shows the four funding sources that have this requirement, along with the matching contribution and the resulting cost that must be provided from another source.

Table 3.6. Funding That Requires a Matching Contribution

Funding Source	Funds Available (in billions of 2018 dollars)	Matching Contribution	Matching Contribution Amount (in billions of 2018 dollars)
DRF PA	37.4	10%	4.2
DRF HMGP	3.0	25%	1.0
Non-DRF appropriations: other	21.2	15%	3.7
Regular federal programs	3.3	15%	0.6
TOTAL	**64.9**		**9.5**

The total of this matching contribution requirement is $9.5 billion. CDBG-DR is a potential source of such funds. If it were to pay for all of the matching contribution requirements, $10.4 billion of its $19.9 billion total would be available for other projects. To the extent that other matching contributions can be found, CDBG-DR funds available for other purposes would increase.

The matching contribution requirement is 25 percent for HMGP and 10 percent for PA, which leads to an estimated cost share of $5.2 billion. Other federal programs have varying requirements, sometimes dependent on very specific details of the project. Using 15 percent as a representative figure for non-DRF appropriations and regular federal programs, plan analysts estimate that $4.3 in matching contributions would be required. These together result in the $9.5 billion total requirement.

The Federal Government as a Potential Funder

A very high level—99.2 percent, or $137.9 billion—of the total cost of the recovery plan is *eligible* for federal funding. This estimate is based on the potential funders list associated with each COA. The lists are reported in the individual sector volumes associated with this project.[8] However, only $85.6 billion of potential federal funding, as well as $8 billion of private insurance, has been identified. Thus, although almost all of the plan costs are eligible for federal funding, a gap remains between our estimate of federal funding available and funds required to implement the recovery plan.

Figure 3.1 shows potential federal agency funding sources by sector. The shaded cells indicate where we identified an agency as a potential funder for any COA in the sector. An early version of this figure, as well as the list of potential agency funders for each COA, was sent to representatives of all the relevant agencies in the July 9, 2018, preliminary draft of the recovery plan.[9] While HSOAC received many comments on many aspects of the recovery plan, there were relatively few comments on this figure. We made appropriate revisions based on the comments that we did receive from the agencies listed.

---

[8] Links to these can be found at RAND Corporation, undated.

[9] It was also released to the public—specifically, posted on the Puerto Rico Central Office of Recovery, Reconstruction, and Resiliency website—the next day for comments. See Central Office of Recovery, Reconstruction, and Resiliency, 2018.

Figure 3.1. Potential Federal Funding Sources, by Sector

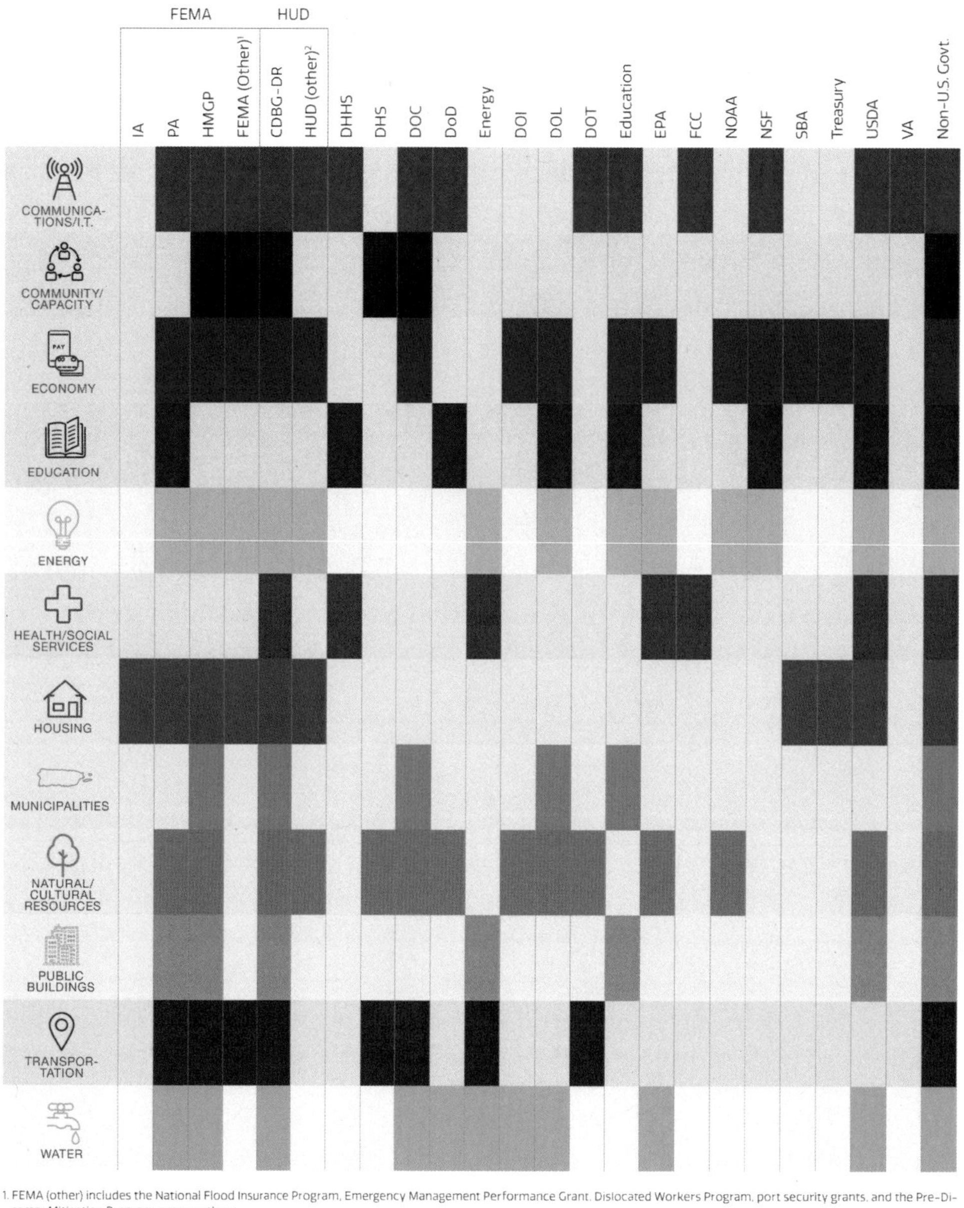

1. FEMA (other) includes the National Flood Insurance Program, Emergency Management Performance Grant, Dislocated Workers Program, port security grants, and the Pre-Disaster Mitigation Program, among others.
2. HUD (other) includes the CDBG Entitlement Program, Capital Fund Program, Rental Assistance Demonstration Program, Choice Neighborhoods Program, Section 18 (Demolition/Disposal), Energy Performance Contracting, and Housing Choice Voucher Program, among others.

SOURCE: Government of Puerto Rico, 2018, p. 170.

Additional Potential Sources of Funding

Because the estimated cost of the plan is $139 billion, and potential estimated funding from the funders identified above is $93.6 billion, at least a $45.4 billion gap remains. If the plan is to be fully funded, additional sources to fund this gap must be found—unless, of course, funding from the sources discussed above increases beyond our estimates. Therefore, we now turn to explore various non–U.S. government sources of funding. These are sources of funding whose total contribution we do not have a good analytical basis for estimating, but which nonetheless should be identified. These include the last five categories of funding sources identified in Table 3.1: the government of Puerto Rico, revenue-generating projects, private-sector funding, philanthropic actors, and local and international NGOs.

Puerto Rico's Contribution

Puerto Rico expects to make a substantial contribution from its own limited resources to support recovery. The recovery plan indicates that the government of Puerto Rico could support many of the COAs at some level. This could include providing personnel, supplies, technical and oversight services, and other critical contributions. We identified over 110 COAs across all sectors, totaling more than $40 billion in costs, to which the government of Puerto Rico could contribute as a primary funder or through matching contributions, which will provide access to certain federal funding sources.

Revenue-Generating Projects

Funding may also come from revenue-generating projects, such as user fees for toll roads, leases, or sale of excess broadband capacity to private companies. While we were not able to assess all the ways in which projects could generate revenues, we identified five COAs (three in the Communications and Information Technology Sector and two in the Transportation Sector) totaling $1.05 billion in costs that would likely be revenue-generating projects. (See also the discussion of P3s below.)

Private-Sector Funding

Puerto Rico is indeed "open for business," and the government encourages private enterprise to invest in projects across the island.[10] Many of the plan's COAs include the private sector as a potential source of funds. We identified more than 50 COAs, totaling more than $40 billion in costs, that are potential candidates for private-sector funding (approximately half of the projects, as well as the costs, are in the Energy Sector). In addition, we identified nearly 20 COAs totaling more than $14 billion in costs that are potential candidates for P3s (primarily in the Natural and Cultural Resources, Transportation, and Water Sectors).

The government of Puerto Rico fully realizes that the projects must be profitable for private investors and is restructuring its processes to be more inviting to private business. In April 2018 the U.S. Department of the Treasury designated Puerto Rico as an Opportunity Zone under the newly enacted Tax Cuts and Jobs Act (Public Law 115-97).[11] Investment in the Opportunity Zone can receive preferential tax treatment, with the goal being to increase such investment.

---

[10] Puerto Rico Department of Economic Development and Commerce, "Governor of Puerto Rico Declared the Island 'Open for Business,' and Invited Investors and Entrepreneurs to Be Part of Its Economic Transformation," Business Wire, February 15, 2018.

[11] U.S. Department of the Treasury, "Treasury, IRS Announce First Round of Opportunity Zones Designations for 18 States," Washington, D.C., April 9, 2018.

Private actors are also, in some cases, themselves taking the lead in increasing their investment in Puerto Rico. Socially responsible business models are seeking to bring targeted investment to hard-hit areas, bringing jobs and capital that, in turn, can benefit rebuilding efforts. Greater private investment may also naturally arise in the aftermath of the storms. Natural disasters can create entrepreneurial opportunities that can in turn spur positive economic and societal outcomes and accelerate recovery.[12] Ten years after Hurricane Katrina, New Orleans had an entrepreneurship rate that was 64 percent higher than the national average and more than double what it was in the year before the disaster.[13]

In addition, private-sector funding could also be generated from institutional investors and P3s.

Institutional investors represent one of the largest categories of potential nongovernmental funding sources—a category that has yet to be systematically tapped for disaster recovery and resilience. The Organisation for Economic Co-operation and Development groups institutional investors into two general categories: "traditional" investors, which include pension funds, investment funds, and insurance companies; and "alternative" investors, which include private equity, sovereign wealth funds, and exchange-traded funds.[14] Though they vary widely in their size, approach, and risk appetite, as a category they control a substantial portion of global assets: between 60 and 70 percent of the shares of medium and large public corporations are held by institutional investors.[15]

Within the broad category of institutional investors, **sovereign wealth funds** (SWFs) are an increasingly important category of investment, representing 6 percent of total global assets.[16] SWFs invest proceeds from national assets—predominantly derived from the export of natural resources—and are controlled by their respective governments.[17] Generally speaking, SWFs have sought investment vehicles that seek to leverage and grow public funds for the long term. They are unique not only in the derivation of their proceeds but also in the incentives that may drive key investment decisions: SWFs are typically aligned with a publicly stated set of investment strategies that guide their use, such as improving domestic infrastructure, weathering

---

[12] Javier Monllor and Nezih Altay, "Discovering Opportunities in Necessity: The Inverse Creative Destruction Effect," *Journal of Small Business and Enterprise Development*, Vol. 23, No. 1, 2016, pp. 274–291; Caroline Baxter Tresise, "How Entrepreneurship Can Support Post-Disaster Recovery," Oxfam, May 25, 2017; Liz Henderson, "The Role of Insurance in Building Resilience," Aon, undated.

[13] Allison Plyer, Nihal Shrinath, and Vicki Mack, "The New Orleans Index at Ten: Measuring Greater New Orleans' Progress Toward Prosperity," The Data Center, July 31, 2015.

[14] Serdar Çelik and Mats Isaksson, "Institutional Investors and Ownership Engagement," *OECD Journal: Financial Market Trends*, Vol. 2013, No. 2, 2014.

[15] Edward B. Rock, "Institutional Investors in Corporate Governance," University of Pennsylvania Law School, Faculty Scholarship Paper 1458, July 21, 2015.

[16] Orinola Gbadebo-Smith, "The Wealth of Nations: Investment Strategies of Sovereign Wealth Funds," Toptal, undated.

[17] Edwin M. Truman, *Sovereign Wealth Funds: Threat or Salvation?* Washington, D.C.: Peterson Institute for International Economics, 2010.

economic shocks, correcting balance of payments, and supporting strategic investments either inside or outside the country.[18] SWFs have also taken on the role of "shareholders of last resort," as evidenced during the financial crisis of 2008.[19] Some SWFs have increasingly sought to diversify their holdings by pursuing new asset classes, including infrastructure. SWF investors from Abu Dhabi, Australia, and Singapore were reported to be interested in making investments in U.S. critical infrastructure, including energy and transportation systems in Puerto Rico after Hurricane Maria.[20]

Some institutional investors already figure prominently in natural disaster response, recovery, and mitigation. For example, traditional financial institutions, including local and regional banks, as well as insurance companies, play a critical role in disaster recovery. Other types of institutional investors, such as SWFs, mutual funds, and hedge funds, have to date played little direct role as investors in natural disaster recovery and hazard mitigation efforts.

In principle, attracting large institutional investors, such as SWFs, into long-term disaster recovery and resilience infrastructure investments may fit well, both as a diversification strategy and as a complement to a broader national infrastructure policy for the target country. Developing and funding resilient infrastructure before a disaster is a role that SWFs could excel at, simultaneously addressing natural disaster risks and building projects capable of returning a profit. If disaster recovery and resilience objectives can be integrated more concretely into an agenda of renewing infrastructure (independent of an actual disaster event having occurred), there may be an opportunity to leverage large-scale capital more effectively to achieve national infrastructure objectives and to prepare communities facing the worsening effects of natural disasters. But this would likely require a more conscious mind-set and policy shift, wherein governments and private investors create a common vision that supports a "merging" of the disaster recovery and resilience infrastructure agenda within broader national and local critical infrastructure objectives.

Several factors may be stifling greater participation on the part of institutional investors. For example, disaster recovery–related investments may not be viewed as strategic or in alignment with institutional goals, particularly for SWFs, when the disaster occurs outside the region. To the extent that disaster recovery and resilience needs are based in fragile economies, the overall investment environment may present political and governance risks that further exacerbate the reticence of institutional investors to engage in those markets.[21] Perhaps the most important

---

[18] Gbadebo-Smith, undated.

[19] Hélène Raymond, "Sovereign Wealth Funds as Domestic Investors of Last Resort During Crises," *International Economics/Economie Internationale*, Vol. 123, 2010, pp. 121–159.

[20] P. K. Semler, "Puerto Rico Becomes Pilot for Trump's $1.5Tn P3 Fund," *Asia Times*, July 2, 2018.

[21] Jeremy Oppenheim and Katherine Stodulka, "Mobilizing Private Infrastructure for Sustainable Finance," paper presented at the Business and Sustainable Development Coalition G20 Brainstorming Workshop, Buenos Aires, September 2017.

reason for a failure to invest in the aftermath of disasters is that risk-return ratios for recovery and resilience projects (and other humanitarian-related investments) simply have not met a threshold acceptable to a larger swath of institutional investors.

These factors notwithstanding, it is possible that shifting conditions are improving the outlook for institutional investor involvement in resilient infrastructure projects. For example, 100 Resilient Cities and the Rockefeller Foundation have begun work on the Urban Resilience Fund, which seeks to facilitate institutional investment in resilient infrastructure projects by establishing market standards and showing the investment value of resilient infrastructure projects.[22]

An uptick in interest in facilitating large investment capital toward disaster recovery and resilience has spurred discussion and action around the application of **public-private partnerships**, or **P3s**, in disaster recovery and resilience. P3s generally function by using some degree of private funds and financing to address public infrastructure needs in exchange for a percentage of future revenue. There are appealing aspects of using P3s when public funding is tight or politically fraught: They can be a viable way of injecting immediate resources into much-needed infrastructure projects. They can add financial flexibility and bring novel corporate innovation and technology to solve infrastructure problems. And they can encourage the timely completion of projects by giving the private partner a profit incentive to avoid delays. P3s also can act to spread the risk across several stakeholders, reducing the burden on government to undertake complex projects.

On the other hand, P3s do not represent "free" money, and there are limitations on when they are appropriate. Even with private financing, the money to recoup project costs must still come from somewhere, either through taxes or user fees.[23] For a project to be feasible, sufficient future revenues must exist (for instance, there must be enough drivers able and willing to pay tolls to justify a new highway or bridge). In disaster-related circumstances, revenue streams can be difficult to come by. P3s can also suffer from a lack of transparency, poor cost sharing and risk sharing, inefficient spending, and overly optimistic revenue projections.[24]

For the most part, a P3 functions best when the process is transparent and accountable, future revenues are sufficient and known, the project benefits the population equitably, and the P3 addresses a fundamental need. In addition, for P3s to function effectively and efficiently, they

---

[22] 100 Resilient Cities, "How to Get Involved," Medium, June 19, 2018.

[23] Kriston Capps, "How Local Governments Came to Embrace Business Partnerships," CityLab, November 10, 2017.

[24] Iliana Ivanova, Oskar Herics, Thomas Obermayr, Pietro Puricella, Enrico Grassi, Guido Fara, Di Hai, Svetoslav Hristov, Maria Carmen Jiménez, Chrysoula Latopoulou, and Maria Ploumaki, *Public Private Partnerships in the EU: Widespread Shortcomings and Limited Benefits*, Luxembourg: European Court of Auditors, European Union, 2018.

should be integrated into a coordinated and centralized plan and be managed by a consistent governing body of leaders and invested stakeholders.[25]

In the United States, P3s are typically executed at the state and municipal level and are subject to a variety of guidelines and requirements. For instance, P3s have been used for the construction of toll road highways, where private companies and banks fund part of the construction costs in exchange for a long-term lease on the toll revenues. The State of Florida opened the Port of Miami Tunnel in 2014, a project built together with a private consortium partner that also serves the concessionaire over a 30-year time frame, with the infrastructure then reverting to the state in 2044.[26] Similarly, the city of Phoenix collaborated with the private sector to design, build, and operate a water treatment plant capable of serving 400,000 homes, at an estimated public cost savings of $30 million.[27]

The Public-Private Partnerships Act of Puerto Rico was passed in 2009, establishing the **Puerto Rico Public-Private Partnerships Authority** in order to "identify innovative measures and nontraditional vehicles that promote and render economic development feasible, provide the People with the required public services, and allow the Government to stabilize its finances."[28] The Public-Private Partnerships Authority has broad powers to identify, evaluate, and select projects carried out by such partnerships. These projects may cover diverse aspects of Puerto Rico's economy, including solid waste facilities (e.g., waste-to-energy and recycling facilities); water and energy infrastructure (e.g., renewable energy projects); transportation infrastructure; health care, educational, law enforcement, and penitentiary facilities; affordable housing; communications infrastructure; and recreational, cultural, and tourism facilities.[29]

Puerto Rico has already implemented several major P3 projects in transportation since the creation of the Puerto Rico Public-Private Partnerships Authority. Luis Muñoz Marín International Airport in San Juan, the largest passenger airport on the island, has been operated since 2013 by Aerostar Airport Holdings, a P3; it is the only major privatized airport in the United States.[30] Two toll roads, PR-5 and PR-22, have been operated by Metropistas, a P3, since

---

[25] Kevin F. McCarthy, *An Economic Development Architecture for New Orleans*, Santa Monica, Calif.: RAND Corporation, TR-547-HI, 2008.

[26] U.S. Department of Transportation, "Port of Miami Tunnel," webpage, undated.

[27] Bipartisan Policy Center, *Bridging the Gap Together: A New Model to Modernize U.S. Infrastructure*, Washington, D.C.: Bipartisan Policy Center, May 2016.

[28] S.B. 469, Act No. 29, Public-Private Partnerships Act of Puerto Rico, Government Bank of Puerto Rico, June 8, 2009.

[29] Government of Puerto Rico, Puerto Rico Public-Private Partnership Authority, "Inventory of Projects," webpage, undated.

[30] Christine Boynton, "Aerostar Airport Holdings Wins Bid for San Juan Airport," *Air Transport World*, July 24, 2012; U.S. Government Accountability Office, *Airport Privatization: Limited Interest Despite FAA's Pilot Program*, Washington, D.C.: U.S. Government Accountability Office, GAO-15-42, November 2014.

2011.[31] Other third-party operations arrangements, such as those of the Teodoro Moscoso Bridge and the Tren Urbano, predate the Public-Private Partnerships Authority, although the Tren Urbano has met with mixed success.[32]

Like P3s, another way to decrease risk and thereby attract large institutional funders is through the use of **blended finance models** whereby developmental, philanthropic, and public funds are merged with investor funds to lower collective risks, scale up projects, and build momentum for more widespread investment.[33] However, blended finance has a broad set of enabling conditions, including governments clearly identifying needs; the articulation of risk mitigation requirements; the channeling and leveraging of private capital for its most effective use; and the ability of NGOs, multilateral development banks, and other key enabling players to strategically support investments. If these conditions are met, various parties may have interest in using blended finance to develop infrastructure projects that meet disaster-related needs.

Philanthropic Actors

In the past few decades, foundations have proliferated globally.[34] There are currently around 85,000 foundations in the United States alone, with an even greater number overseas.[35] A large percentage of those are **charitable foundations**—that is, noncorporate foundations whose primary function is philanthropic. Many charitable foundations are family foundations, giving away personal or inherited wealth. Others are community foundations, pooling resources of many people within a region to maximize their impact. For Puerto Rico's recovery plan, we identified over 40 COAs totaling more than $10 billion in costs for which nongovernmental sources may contribute where federal funding or other sources do not fully meet a need (many of these projects are in the Education, Health and Social Services, and Natural and Cultural Resources sectors). While philanthropic actors will not cover most of these costs, they may identify specific needs that align with their interests and capabilities to make a meaningful contribution to Puerto Rico's recovery.

Disaster response, recovery, and mitigation represents a significant commitment of charitable foundations, though it can take various forms. For example, many foundations seek to address

---

[31] Federal Highway Administration, Center for Innovative Finance Support, "Project Profile: Puerto Rico PR-22 and PR-5 Lease," undated.

[32] U.S. Department of Transportation, "Teodoro Moscoso Bridge, San Juan, Puerto Rico," webpage, last updated September 9, 2014; Federal Transit Administration, *The Predicted and Actual Impacts of New Starts Projects—2007: Capital Cost and Ridership*, Washington, D.C.: Federal Transit Administration, April 2008.

[33] Paul Horrocks, Wiebke Bartz-Zuccala, Irene Basile, Naeeda Crishna Morgado, Jens Sedemund, Julia Benn, Cécile Sangare, and Tomas Hos, *Blended Finance: Mobilising Resources for Sustainable Development and Climate Action in Developing Countries*, Paris: Organisation for Economic Co-operation and Development, October 2017.

[34] For the purposes of this report, "charitable foundations" refers to NGOs that provide funding to other organizations or fund their own projects—generally focusing on philanthropic or humanitarian efforts.

[35] Stanley Weinstein and Pamela Barden, *The Complete Guide to Fundraising Management*, 4th ed., Hoboken, N.J.: John Wiley and Sons, 2017; Susan U. Raymond, *Recession, Recovery, and Renewal: Long-Term Nonprofit Strategies for Rapid Economic Change*, Hoboken, N.J.: John Wiley and Sons, 2013.

the issue indirectly by focusing on climate change, economic resilience, and community revitalization. For instance, the Ford Foundation's contribution to the $5 million Reimagine Puerto Rico project aims to help Puerto Rico rebuild while also supporting the foundation's focus on reducing global inequality.[36] Others engage in direct disaster relief, bringing in food, water, medicine, energy, or temporary housing in the aftermath of storms, floods, earthquakes, and fires. In 2015, more than $75 million was contributed to worldwide natural disaster relief efforts by the largest U.S. charitable foundations.[37]

One area where charitable foundations can have a major impact is in efforts to build more resilient communities and develop sustainable infrastructure. The Rockefeller Foundation's 100 Resilient Cities initiative, for example, seeks to improve disaster mitigation and resilience planning for cities worldwide by bringing resources and expertise to municipalities facing concrete disaster risks.[38]

Corporate giving for disaster recovery has burgeoned since the 2004 Indian Ocean earthquake and tsunami, and can come in many forms, with some companies directing their philanthropy through corporate foundations, while others provide funds directly through their corporate social responsibility arms.[39] In the face of natural disasters, some companies give cash, send supplies, or coordinate the use of their employees as volunteers or as targeted problem solvers to take advantage of the company's area of expertise.

Corporate foundations are most likely to invest in rebuilding efforts that help achieve corporate goals, improve corporate reputation, or do both. For instance, a corporate foundation for a telecommunications company might fund projects bringing broadband internet to rural areas. The foundation might also fund other types of projects, such as building schools and scholarships, to gain broader visibility and recognition in the community. Companies can also look to humanitarian philanthropy as a testing ground for new innovations, from using drones to deliver vaccines and lifesaving medicine to using solar-powered balloons to restore internet access to Puerto Rico after Hurricane Maria.[40]

---

[36] Ford Foundation, "Foundations Commit $5M to Ensure an Equitable Recovery in Puerto Rico," New York, November 16, 2017.

[37] Cindy Cario, Andrew Grabois, Naomi Henry, Supriya Kumar, Lawrence T. McGill, Darya Oreshkina, Betty Saronson, Grace Sato, Kathy Gutowsky, Robert G. Ottenhoff, and Regine A. Webster, *Measuring the State of Disaster Philanthropy*, New York: Foundation Center and Center for Disaster Philanthropy, 2017.

[38] 100 Resilient Cities, "About Us," webpage, undated.

[39] Many companies do both, depending—among other factors—on tax implications.

[40] Tony Morain, "Direct Relief, Merck and Partners Test Temperature-Controlled Autonomous Drone Delivery System for Medicines in Puerto Rico," Direct Relief, August 24, 2018; Alastair Westgarth, "Turning on Project Loon in Puerto Rico," Medium, October 20, 2017.

U.S. companies contributed more than $400 million in relief for five major natural disasters in 2017 and gave over $20 billion in that year to philanthropic causes generally.[41] After Hurricane Maria, AbbVie, a pharmaceutical company with a substantial presence in Puerto Rico, pledged $100 million to the recovery effort.[42] Corporate aid can be critical, providing logistical and support assistance, as well as funding.[43] After Hurricane Katrina, Walmart took advantage of its supply chain expertise to get trucks filled with crucial supplies to New Orleans, sometimes beating FEMA to certain locations.[44] Companies can also contribute after a disaster via direct investment, both bolstering current operations and infusing capital into new projects.

With their ability to drive economic recovery, create jobs, maximize technology, and improve accountability, corporations can provide unique value both before and after a disaster that governments cannot easily duplicate.[45] For example, after Hurricane Katrina, the city of New Orleans was losing more than $15 million a day in tourism revenue—as a result, a number of companies and business associations made a point of holding conventions and events in New Orleans, helping the sector rebound.[46]

Individual donations account for 80 percent of all humanitarian giving.[47] In the disaster context, individual postdisaster contributions generally amount to more than foundation giving, corporate philanthropy, and bequests combined.[48] Twenty major nonprofits reported receiving more than $160 million in Hurricane Maria–related funding from over 350,000 individuals in the months of August–December 2017.[49] Much of those funds are directed, in turn, to NGOs. For instance, of the $41 million raised by the Unidos por Puerto Rico campaign from 135,000 individuals, more than $39 million was directed to NGOs operating in Puerto Rico.[50]

---

[41] Giving USA, *Giving USA 2018: The Annual Report on Philanthropy for the Year 2017*, Chicago: Giving USA Foundation and Indiana University Lilly Family School of Philanthropy, 2018, p. 156 (more than $400 million in relief for five major natural disasters in 2017) and p. 147 (over $20 billion in that year to philanthropic causes generally).

[42] AbbVie, "AbbVie Donates $100 Million to Strengthen Access to Healthcare, Housing for Hurricane-Ravaged Puerto Rico," May 22, 2018.

[43] Alan Muller and Gail Whiteman, "Exploring the Geography of Corporate Philanthropic Disaster Response: A Study of Fortune Global 500 Firms," *Journal of Business Ethics*, Vol. 84, No. 4, 2009, pp. 589–603.

[44] Devin Leonard, "The Only Lifeline Was the Wal-Mart," *Fortune*, October 3, 2005, pp. 74–80; Ann Zimmerman, and Valerie Bauerlein, "At Wal-Mart, Emergency Plan Has Big Payoff," *Wall Street Journal*, September 12, 2005.

[45] Julie Belanger, David Sharrock, Hiroko Araki, Tensai Asfaw, David Matern, Silvanus Okumu, Ekaterina Papaioannou, Lisbeth Pilegaard, and Siti Kamariah Ahmad Subki, *High-Level Panel on Humanitarian Financing: Too Important to Fail—Addressing the Humanitarian Financing Gap*, New York: United Nations, January 2016.

[46] Business Civic Leadership Center, *Business Disaster Assistance and Recovery, Second Report: Long-Term Recovery Issues and Case Studies*, Washington, D.C.: Business Civic Leadership Center, August 2007.

[47] Belanger et al., 2016.

[48] Sarah Breitenbach, "Nonprofits Poised for Bigger Role in Disaster Recovery," Pew Charitable Trusts, June 23, 2017; Giving USA, 2018.

[49] Sara Nason, *One Year Later: Hurricane Maria*, Glen Rock, N.J.: Charity Navigator, 2018.

[50] Unidos por Puerto Rico, "Donations in Action," webpage, undated.

While major gifts from **high-net-worth donors** are responsible for some of the philanthropic output by individuals, much of it is made up of small-scale contributions from large numbers of people.[51] Two-thirds of Americans give charitably every year.[52] The average amount of charitable giving in the United States in 2015 was just over $2,000 per household, with high-net-worth donors giving an average of approximately $25,000 apiece.[53] Overall, individual giving to charity stood at more than $285 billion as of 2017.[54]

A large number of global billionaires have also signed the Giving Pledge—a commitment by the signatories to give away at least half of their wealth in their lifetimes or in their wills.[55] Among high-net-worth individuals in general, only 8 percent reported that disaster relief was one of the three most important charitable issues for them.[56] With a large Puerto Rican population living and thriving on CONUS, many globally prominent Puerto Ricans gave and raised money in the aftermath of Hurricane Maria.[57]

Beyond high-net-worth contributions, **small-scale individual giving** can add up to very large dollar amounts. While small-scale donations have traditionally been diffuse, emerging technology is starting to enable individual donors to have impacts that rival those of large philanthropists. Online giving is now the leading choice of individuals wishing to donate to disaster relief.[58] Crowdfunding is increasingly being used to solicit individual donations, often to great effect; after the 2015 earthquake in Nepal, more than $20 million was raised through crowdfunding sites.[59] In Puerto Rico, the crowdfunding site GlobalGiving had raised nearly $12 million for Hurricane Maria disaster relief from over 61,000 contributions as of March

---

[51] Karl Zinsmeister, "The Philanthropy of the Little Guys," *World*, March 10, 2018.

[52] Vickie An, "Small Donation, Big Impact: What You Need to Know About Microgiving," *Forbes*, November 13, 2015.

[53] The 2016 U.S. Trust Study, from which these numbers are drawn, defines high-net-worth individuals as those with a net worth of more than $1 million (excluding the value of their primary residences) and/or those with an income of greater than $200,000 a year. In the study the average net worth of the respondents was just under $17 million. U.S. Trust, *The 2016 U.S. Trust Study of High Net Worth Philanthropy: Charitable Practices and Preferences of Wealthy Households*, New York: U.S. Trust and Indiana University Lilly Family School of Philanthropy, October 2016.

[54] National Philanthropic Trust, "Charitable Giving Statistics," webpage, undated; Giving USA, 2018.

[55] The Giving Pledge, "A Commitment to Philanthropy," homepage, undated; Bill Gates, "Why Inequality Matters," Gatesnotes: The Blog of Bill Gates, October 13, 2014.

[56] U.S. Trust, 2016.

[57] Veronica Villafañe, "Jennifer Lopez, Daddy Yankee Donate $1 Million to Puerto Rico; Maná Gives $200,000 to Aid Mexico," *Forbes*, September 25, 2017.

[58] Giving USA, 2018, p. 78.

[59] Devin Thorpe, "In Under 60 Days, Crowdfunding Sites Raise over $20 Million for Nepal Relief," *Forbes*, June 12, 2015.

2019,[60] while pop star Ricky Martin raised an additional $4.6 million for his native Puerto Rico through the crowdfunding site YouCaring.[61]

Local and International NGOs

Estimates put the number of NGOs operating worldwide at roughly 10 million.[62] While many NGOs are enormous, globe-spanning organizations with tens of thousands of employees and volunteers, the majority of NGOs are small and local.[63] NGOs can bring a tremendous amount of value to disaster relief, from money, equipment, and service capacity to data, relationships, and expertise.[64]

NGOs have several benefits compared with other actors. By being nested in the community, many NGOs can be uniquely positioned to contribute to community development and resilience building.[65] NGOs can relay information about a disaster zone back to the rest of the world and raise the profile of a disaster, thereby bringing in greater resources. NGOs can also often act faster than any other actors, and can sometimes impartially gain access where political instability limits the role of others.[66]

The position of **local NGOs**, embedded within communities, means that their relief effort often begins immediately, while outside organizations are still getting organized. In the weeks and months after Hurricane Katrina, evidence suggests that faith-based organizations and NGOs throughout the affected region took the lead in providing shelter, food, medical care, childcare, and other services for countless people—often forming the only lifeline some residents had after the storms. A 2006 Homeland Security Institute report states,

> The scale of their response was unprecedented. In some communities, they—not the government—were the focal point for services. In other communities, they

[60] Disaster Recovery Network at GlobalGiving, "Puerto Rico & Caribbean Hurricane Relief Fund," GlobalGiving, undated.

[61] Giving USA, 2018, p. 79.

[62] Nonprofit Action, "Facts and Stats About NGOs Worldwide," webpage, September 4, 2015.

[63] Jeffrey J. Stys, "Non-Profit Involvement in Disaster Response and Recovery," paper prepared for the Center for Law, Environment, Adaptation and Resources, University of North Carolina School of Law, January 17, 2011.

[64] Joie D. Acosta, Anita Chandra, and Jeanne Ringel, "Nongovernmental Resources to Support Disaster Preparedness, Response and Recovery," *Disaster Medicine and Public Health Preparedness*, Vol. 7, No. 4, August 2013, pp. 348–353.

[65] Anita Chandra and Joie Acosta, *The Role of Nongovernmental Organizations in Long-Term Human Recovery After Disaster: Reflections from Louisiana Four Years After Hurricane Katrina*, Santa Monica, Calif.: RAND Corporation, OP-277-RC, 2009.

[66] Yukie Osa, "The Growing Role of NGOs in Disaster Relief and Humanitarian Assistance in East Asia," in Rizal Sukma and James Gannon, eds., *A Growing Force: Civil Society's Role in Asian Regional Security*, Tokyo: Japan Center for International Exchange, 2013, pp. 66–89; Pete Hull, Stephen Bowen, Tanya Buttress, Bridget Kanawati, Russell Miller, Richard Rowe, Sarah Maloney, and John Sopko, *Heralding Unheard Voices: The Role of Faith-Based Organizations and Nongovernmental Organizations During Disasters, Final Report*, Arlington, Va.: Homeland Security Institute, December 18, 2006.

were the sole or lead provider of services for days or weeks. They made life-and-death differences in people's lives.[67]

NGOs generally also have the benefit of being established in the community. They maintain good relationships with local officials and are often in contact with vulnerable populations, who are in particular need of help after a disaster.[68] On the other hand, those NGOs working in the community (and their employees and volunteers) may also be affected, along with the rest of the community, after a disaster—perhaps lacking power, water, transportation, or means of communication themselves.

In the aftermath of Hurricane Maria, countless local NGOs provided essential services to communities throughout Puerto Rico.[69] The nonprofit Asociación Recreativa y Educativa Comunal Barrio Mariana, Inc. (ARECMA), for instance, helped clear debris, provided meals to those without power and water, and acted as a hub for relief operations in the immediate aftermath of the storms. Later in the recovery process, ARECMA established solar-powered laundry facilities, a repository of tools and machinery, and developed a business incubator.[70] Local NGOs Resilient Power Puerto Rico and Para la Naturaleza installed rainwater purification and solar power systems to keep community centers operational,[71] while the Foundation for Puerto Rico provided aid to farmers; distributed medical supplies, solar lamps, water filters, mosquito repellent and larvicide; and set up Wi-Fi antennas to provide connectivity for 2,000 users.[72] Going forward, local NGOs could play critical roles in bringing expertise and capacity to addressing COAs identified in the plan.

Of course, not all NGOs are small, local, or permanent fixtures in the communities in which they operate. Many **international NGOs** who are active in disaster response, like Catholic Charities, Habitat for Humanity, or the Red Cross, are global institutions with budgets as large as Fortune 500 companies. At the same time, some of the largest NGOs maintain a permanent local presence in many places at once. The American Red Cross, for instance, with roughly $3.5 billion in assets, has supplies and staff positioned across the United States, able to deploy emergency supplies anywhere in the country within 24 hours.[73] International NGOs bring tremendous

---

[67] Hull et al., 2006.

[68] Stys, 2011.

[69] Isabel Beltrán, "One Year Later: The Critical Role of NGOs in Puerto Rico's Recovery," 100 Resilient Cities, September 20, 2018.

[70] "Extreme Conditions Spur Innovative Community Response," Unidos por Puerto Rico, February 20, 2019.

[71] Adele Peters, "During Puerto Rico's Blackout, Solar Microgrids Kept the Lights On," *Fast Company*, April 24, 2018.

[72] Foundation for Puerto Rico, "Foundation for Puerto Rico Hurricane Maria Relief Fund," webpage, undated.

[73] Brian Clontz, Doug Stockham, and Ryan Raffin, "Lessons Learned from Recent Natural Disaster Relief Funds: Part 1 of 3," Planned Giving Design Center, April 21, 2015; KPMG LLP, *The American National Red Cross: Consolidated Financial Statements*, McLean, Va.: KPMG LLP, June 30, 2015.

experience and expertise to postdisaster response and recovery and could conceivably be invaluable in helping to directly address COAs in terms of knowledge, personnel, and resources.

Identifying Potential Funding Sources for Each Course of Action

In support of the recovery plan, HSOAC identified potential funders for each COA; see the individual sector volumes associated with this project for more information.[74] For federal agencies, we did this only at the agency level (cabinet department or equivalent), as shown in Figure 3.1. Each agency has many programs, and we judged that trying to identify all the programs in an agency that would be potential funders of each COA would not be practical. Whether a specific COA is eligible for funding from a specific program depends on the kinds of activities required to carry out the COA and on the program's eligibility rules. These rules vary both in their goals and in the costs they will cover, and they have specific eligibility requirements for both applicants and projects. Determining the extent to which recovery plan COAs conform to those requirements will require more detailed analysis, as well as federal agency review. Several federal program managers participated in discussions during the development of the COAs, but they said that they could not judge the funding eligibility of specific activities without reviewing program applications. Both the time constraints of the project and the early stages of planning—prior to the development of specific implementation plans—would not allow for a comprehensive identification of all potential federal program funders for each COA.

We judged that a noncomprehensive list of potential programs might well mistakenly be interpreted to mean that other programs were not potential funders, and thus be dangerously misleading to readers. We also judged that no matter how many caveats we included (such as, "This is not necessarily the complete list") we would still run this risk. Even for programs that we believed would be good potential funders, we judged that we could only responsibly identify them as such after we had conferred with representatives of such a program. It could well turn out that we were wrong in our judgment, and this would also make the list misleading. Again, the time constraints on our work and early stages of recovery planning precluded this. Thus, we erred on the side of caution, and only listed potential funders at the agency level. It will be the responsibility of those in Puerto Rico who are implementing the plan to determine the appropriate programs from which to obtain funding.

For additional information on potential recovery resources, plan implementers can consult FEMA's National Disaster Recovery Framework[75] and the U.S. General Services

---

[74] Links to these can be found at RAND Corporation, undated.

[75] See FEMA, "National Disaster Recovery Framework," webpage, undated.

Administration's Catalog of Federal Domestic Assistance—the most comprehensive source of information on all federal assistance programs.[76]

Constructing a Complete Funding Matrix: Identifying Specific Funders for Each COA

Finally, we considered constructing such a matrix. We judged, and FEMA concurred, that this was not a useful exercise at this time for the following reasons.

Total funding that Puerto Rico will receive from all sources, both DRF and supplementals, ongoing federal programs and non-U.S. government sources, is *currently uncertain*, so there is no hard dollar constraint to use for such a matrix. While we judged it useful to estimate the total amounts available from some sources so that we could get a useful characterization of the challenge of how many resources still had to be found, we did not judge that this was an appropriate basis for a specific, COA-by-COA distribution.

Specifically, total funding estimated to be available—from the sources for which we could estimate—is less than the total recovery plan cost. If we were to allocate only the funding for which we had those estimated values, only some COAs would be funded, and some would not. This would require an assessment (at least implicit) of *the relative value of COAs*. We had no basis on which do so in this work; the plan was designed as an integral whole. Further, we did *not solicit commitments* from non-U.S. government sources, so it would be inappropriate to say, "Organization *X* will pay for COA *Y*."

Since some COAs are candidates for multiple funding sources, there are *many combinations of funders* that could support any plan. Thus, it is now indeterminate as to which agency would support which COA, and any specific allocation at this time would be too arbitrary to be useful as a policy guide.

Chapter Summary

This chapter has identified potential funders and discussed a framework for allocating funding sources to individual COAs in Puerto Rico's recovery plan. We considered the merits of differing levels of detail in doing a funding analysis. We first identified potential funding sources and the dollar value of their contribution to the recovery plan. Then we more specifically identified potential funding sources for each COA. However, we did not construct a complete funding plan, which would indicate what organizations will fund how much of the costs of each COA. We judged, and FEMA concurred, that constructing such a plan would not be useful at this early stage of the recovery process. One reason is the large gap between estimated plan cost and funding amounts currently identified. Allocating the funding available would necessarily fund only a subset of the total plan, which would require an assessment (at least implicit) of the

---

[76] U.S. General Services Administration, *2018 Catalog of Federal Domestic Assistance*, Washington, D.C.: U.S. General Services Administration, November 2018.

relative value of COAs. We had no basis on which do so; the plan was designed as an integral whole.

The primary funding sources identified include federal government sources, such as the DRF, other appropriations made for disaster relief in legislation, and regular ongoing federal programs. A very high level (99.2 percent) of the total cost of the recovery plan is *eligible* for federal funding, however, a gap remains between our estimate of potential federal funding available ($85.6 billion) and funds required to implement the recovery plan ($139 billion). Proceeds from private insurance ($8 billion) will also cover some costs. Additional funding contributions will come from government of Puerto Rico entities, at either the commonwealth or municipal level, and proceeds from COAs that are revenue-generating projects. Some funders, particularly certain federal programs, will fund only a percentage of any project and require a matching contribution. As such, many COAs will necessarily have more than one funder.

We identified $93.6 billion in potential estimated funding available for Puerto Rico. The largest sources of funding include the DRF, primarily FEMA PA grants and other appropriations, such as CDBG-DR funds. Of this total, $64.9 million of federal funds can only be accessed with a matching contribution. The total amount of the required matching contribution is $9.5 billion. The CDBG-DR is a potential source of such funds, but to the extent that other matching contributions can be found, these funds would remain available for other purposes. In addition, the government of Puerto Rico projects that $8 billion will be available in insurance proceeds. Because the estimated cost of the plan is $139 billion, and potential estimated funding is $93.6 billion, a $45.4 billion gap remains. If the plan is to be fully funded, additional sources to fund this gap must be found.

While their level is currently uncertain, contributions will come from nongovernmental sources, such as private-sector funding and philanthropic actors. Some investors already figure prominently in natural disaster response, recovery, and mitigation. However, several factors may be stifling greater participation on the part of certain classes of investors; these include a lack of alignment with strategic or institutional goals, political and governance risks, and risk-return ratios for recovery and resilience projects. P3s can be a viable way of injecting immediate resources into much-needed infrastructure projects, adding financial flexibility and bringing corporate innovation and technology. However, there may be limitations to P3 due to project feasibility, lack of transparency, poor cost sharing and risk sharing, and imprecise revenue projections.

While philanthropic actors will not cover most of the costs, they may identify specific needs that align with their interests and capabilities to make a meaningful contribution to Puerto Rico's recovery. For example, one area where charitable foundations can have a major impact is in efforts to build more resilient communities and develop sustainable infrastructure. Corporate giving in the face of natural disasters has increased in the last decade and can take the form of cash, supplies, or coordination of employees as volunteers or targeted problem solvers. Individual donations are the primary source of humanitarian giving; however, few high-net-worth individuals generally identify disaster relief as one of the most important issues for them. Nonetheless, many globally prominent Puerto Ricans have donated and raised money in the aftermath of Hurricane Maria. Small-scale individual giving can also add up to large dollar amounts, and online giving is now the leading choice of individuals wishing to donate to disaster relief. Since Hurricane Maria struck, countless local NGOs provided essential services to communities throughout Puerto Rico. Being established in the community, many NGOs can be uniquely positioned to contribute to community development and capacity building, relay information about a disaster area to the rest of the world, and act faster than other actors, in part because they are often in contact with vulnerable populations who are in particular need of help after a disaster. On the other hand, local NGOs may also be affected, along with the rest of the community, after a disaster. Larger, international NGOs bring tremendous experience and expertise to postdisaster response and recovery and could also conceivably help directly address COAs in terms of knowledge, personnel, and resources.

Appendix to Chapter 3: A More Formal Approach to Funding Analysis

In this appendix we present a more formal approach to assigning funding sources to COAs.[77] We have argued in the body of this chapter that it is not useful at this stage of the recovery process to make an explicit allocation of funding sources to specific COAs; hence, we will not apply this approach to the current Puerto Rico recovery plan. However, at some point this kind of allocation will inevitably be done. We expect that the approach described here could usefully be implemented in the future—likely as a supplemental tool to support other approaches to allocations—so we present it here.

We first repeat our characterization of a funding plan from earlier in this chapter: A complete funding plan would indicate what organizations will fund how much of the costs of each COA. We can most easily think of it as a *funding matrix*, in which the rows represent COAs, or parts of COAs, and the columns represent funding organizations. Each element of the matrix would be the amount of each COA or part of a COA that is paid for by each funding organization. The sum across each row would be total funding going toward the associated COA or part of a COA. The sum down each column would be the total funding from each funding organization. The total of all cells in the matrix would, of course, be the total cost of the recovery program that is funded.

We now present a more formal mathematical programming approach to the issue of how to assign funding sources to COA and cost category combinations. In a complex real-world situation, there are many different funders, each willing to fund some, but not all, of many COA and cost category combinations. The most appropriate allocation of funders to these combinations, in the sense of maximizing COA achievement, will not be readily apparent.

If total funding resources available *exceed* the total cost of all COAs, this does not ensure that all the COAs can in fact be funded: the constraints on which COA and cost category combinations funders will fund may make achieving total funding of all COAs impossible. In this case, the mathematical programming approach can in theory find the allocation that maximizes *COA achievement*, which may be simply defined as total spending on all COAs. Alternately, it could be a complex function of funding on each COA. The function might not weigh funding on the COAs equally, and it could be convex or concave in the amount spent on each COA. In general, in this appendix we will represent COA achievement as total spending on all COAs, but we will refer to other formulations at times.

If total funding resources available *are less than* the total cost of all COAs, the allocation that maximizes COA achievement may nonetheless not exhaust all the available funds. This is also because of constraints on what COA and cost category combinations funders will fund. Thus, in both cases a mathematical programming approach can aid decisionmakers in making the best decisions about what funders to assign to what COA and cost category combinations.

---

[77] We gratefully acknowledge the contribution of our RAND colleague Jeremy Eckhause, who independently developed an approach to funding allocation similar to ours. We have freely drawn from his work.

The programming approach answers two questions: Given the following—

- a set of COAs, each with a set of costs in various categories, the sum of which is the *cost of the COA*
- a set of funders, each with a total budget
- a set of rules that indicates, for each COA and cost category combination, whether it is eligible or not for funding from any given funder
- a set of matching-contribution requirements for each funder
- a set of rules on whether each funder will or will not pay matching-contribution requirements

—is there an allocation of funders to COA and cost category combinations so that all COA costs are covered? If not, what is the best we can do, given a value function over COA achievement?

We will first present a linear programming representation of the problem. We will then discuss the limitations of this approach—that is, what real-world issues it abstracts from, and how to modify the program to appropriately address those issues. Each step in such a modification process increases the fidelity of the model and also increases its complexity and its difficulty of solution.

A Linear Formulation of the Problem

In this formulation *COA achievement* means total spending on COAs in any cost category. We define the following variables (a complete table of all the variables in this appendix, and their definitions, is included as Table 3.7 later in this appendix):

- as in the Appendix to Chapter 2, r $(r = 1, \dots, NR)$ is an index of the NR COAs
- also as in the Appendix to Chapter 2, $C(r)$ is the cost of carrying out COA r at its maximum level
- NJ is the number of COA cost categories
- j $(j = 1, \dots, NJ)$ is an index of the COA cost categories
- $\gamma(r,j)$ is the cost of COA r in category j, so

$$C(r) = \sum_{j=1}^{NJ} \gamma(r,j) \tag{3.1}$$

is the total cost of COA r.

Next we define variables related to funding:

- NF is the number of potential funders.
- f $(f = 1, \dots, NF)$ is an index of potential funders.
- $F(f)$ is the total funding available from funder f.

We distinguish between what we will call *primary* and *matching-contribution* funding. As discussed above, some funders will only fund a certain portion of a project's cost, and they then require the recipient of the funds to find the rest (called the matching contribution) elsewhere. We define the following additional variables:

- $X(r,j,f)$ is the primary funding for cost category j of COA r that is provided by funder f.
- $m(r,j,f)$ is a parameter, the maximum percent of $\gamma(r,j)$ that funder f will provide.

Thus, if the funder will fund only 75 percent of the cost of an activity, m is 0.75.

$$X(r,j,f) \leq m(r,j,f)\gamma(r,j) \qquad \forall\, r,j,f. \tag{3.2}$$

- $a(r,j,f)$ is a parameter that has value 1 if category j of the cost of COA r is eligible for primary funding from funder f, and 0 if not.

Total primary funding expenditure by funder f, $\Xi(f)$ is then

$$\Xi(f) = \sum_{r=1}^{NR} \sum_{j=1}^{NJ} a(r,j,f)X(r,j,f). \tag{3.3}$$

We multiply $X(r,j,f)$ by $a(r,j,f)$ to ensure that there will be no spending by a funder on ineligible parts of COAs. Any such spending on ineligible parts of COAs would not count toward meeting COA costs, and thus not contribute to the objective function. Therefore, such spending will not be part of the solution to the program.

Some funders will provide matching-contribution funding, and some will not. We define the following variables related to matching contributions:

- $Y(r,j,f)$ is the matching contribution for cost category j of COA r that is provided by funder f.
- $b(r,j,f)$ is a parameter that has value 1 if category j of the cost of COA r is eligible for matching-contribution funding from funder f, and 0 if not.

Total matching-contribution funding by funder f, $\Upsilon(f)$ is then

$$\Upsilon(f) = \sum_{r=1}^{NR} \sum_{j=1}^{NJ} b(r,j,f)Y(r,j,f). \tag{3.4}$$

We multiply $Y(r,j,f)$ by $b(r,j,f)$ for the same reason that we multiply $X(r,j,f)$ by $a(r,j,f)$.

If a COA and cost category primary funding source has a matching-contribution requirement, we require that sufficient matching contributions are actually provided. As an example, say a primary funder will fund only 75 percent of the cost of an activity and requires that the other 25 percent of the cost be provided as a matching contribution from another source. The linear program then requires that the matching contribution of 25 percent of the cost (one-third of the primary funder's expenditure) actually be made. This formulation does allow multiple primary funders, each doing part of the total, so long as sufficient matching contributions are made corresponding to each one.

$$\sum_{f=1}^{NF} \mu(r,j,f)a(r,j,f)X(r,j,f) \leq \sum_{f=1}^{NF} b(r,j,f)Y(r,j,f) \qquad \forall r,j \tag{3.5}$$

$$\mu(r,j,f) = [\frac{(1 - m(r,j,f)]}{m(r,j,f)}. \tag{3.6}$$

Here, if the funder will fund only 75 percent of the cost of an activity, m is 0.75, and μ is one-third.

The constraint that no funder can expend more than its available funds is

$$\Xi(f) + \Upsilon(f) \leq F(f) \qquad \forall f. \tag{3.7}$$

Finally, we define total spending on cost category j of COA r as $S(r,j)$.

$$S(r,j) = \sum_{f=1}^{NF} [a(r,j,f)X(r,j,f) + b(r,j,f)Y(r,j,f)] \qquad \forall r,j \tag{3.8}$$

The constraint that no more can be spent on cost category j of COA r than its full cost is

$$S(r,j) \leq \gamma(r,j) \qquad \forall r,j \tag{3.9}$$

The objective function, to be maximized, is simply

$$\sum_{r=1}^{NR} \sum_{j=1}^{NJ} S(r,j). \tag{3.10}$$

That is, it is all spending on COAs.

All Variables

Table 3.7 presents all variables in this appendix.

Table 3.7. Names and Definitions of Variables

Name	Definition
NR	Number of COAs in the recovery plan (276, in this case).
$r\ (r = 1, \ldots, NR)$	An index over the COAs.
$C(r)$	The cost of carrying out COA r at its maximum level.
NJ	Number of COA cost categories.
$j\ (j = 1, \ldots, NJ)$	An index of COA cost categories.
$\gamma(r,j)$	The cost of COA r in category j.
NF	Number of potential funders.
$f\ (f = 1, \ldots, NF)$	An index of potential funders.
$F(f)$	Total funding available from funder f.
$X(r,j,f)$	Primary funding for cost category j of COA r that is provided by funder f.
$m(r,j,f)$	The maximum percent of $\gamma(r,j)$ that funder f will provide.
$a(r,j,f)$	A parameter with value 1 if category j of the cost of COA r is eligible for primary funding from funder f, and 0 if not.
$\Xi(f)$	Total primary funding expenditure by funder f.
$Y(r,j,f)$	Matching contribution for cost category j of COA r that is provided by funder f.
$b(r,j,f)$	A parameter with value 1 if category j of the cost of COA r is eligible for matching-contribution funding from funder f, and 0 if not.
$\Upsilon(f)$	Total matching-contribution funding by funder f.
$\mu(r,j,f)$	A parameter defined by $\mu(r,j,f) = [(1 - m(r,j,f)]/m(r,j,f)$.
$S(r,j)$	Total spending on cost category j of COA r.

Improvements to the Formulation

The linear programming formulation given in this appendix does not capture many real-world issues, and many improvements could be made. First, there is no temporal dimension in the problem. As discussed in the body of the chapter, some cost categories are incurred only after others have been, as in the example of operations cost depending on how much construction cost has been achieved. In addition, binary COAs—that is, ones that only have value if fully funded—cannot be represented in the linear model. A mixed-integer approach would be needed to represent this, in which the COA has a given value if it is fully funded, and a zero value at any lower funding level.

Another improvement to the objective function would be that the *value* of achieving one cost category in COA r may depend on how much of the others are achieved. This would imply a nonlinear objective function. Nonlinearity in valuation may extend across COAs, as well as within them. If any COAs value increases with the level of achievement of others, the objective function is convex, with its attendant difficulty of solution. For example, in the formulation of the recovery plan, some COAs are characterized as *foundational*—that is, the value of other COAs depends on the foundational ones being achieved.

In Chapter 2 and its appendix we discussed how the *cost* of one COA may depend on the level of achievement of others. The absorptive capacity issue is one manifestation of this; it cannot be represented in the linear model. In this case, increases in the level of one COA will increase the cost of others. There may also be cases in which COAs can jointly use some capacity (such as ditches for communications and power lines); here increases in the level of one COA will decrease the cost of others.

This approach assumes that the willingness of a funder to pay a matching contribution is independent of which funder is paying the primary amount, which may not be true. It also assumes that any COA and cost category combination can be funded by a combination of funders. It does not restrict the number of primary funders of any given COA and cost category combination, so long as no primary funder funds more than its own maximum share of the total cost, $m(r, j, f)$, and matching contributions are found for all. Imposing restrictions on the number of funders per COA would add more integer constraints to the problem.

We cannot judge at this time what the "right" level of complexity is for any specific implementation of this approach. Those responsible for plan implementation will have to make that determination, weighing the costs and benefits of differing levels of complexity.

A Simple Example

We illustrate the linear programming model with a simple example. It is instructive to try to manually find assignments of funders to COAs that meet all the constraints in this simple model; it is a representative example of the much larger actual real-world problem.

The simple model has the following components:

- There are five COAs and only one cost category per COA.

COA Name	COA 1	COA 2	COA 3	COA 4	COA 5	Total
Cost	10	20	30	40	50	150

- There are five funders. Each may or may not require a matching contribution, and each may or may not be willing to pay matching contributions required by others. The required matching contribution is shown in the third row of the matrix below as a percent. If a funder requires a matching contribution, it is the same for any COA. Funders willing to pay matching contributions will do so for any COA.

Funder	CDBG-DR	PA	Dept A	Dept B	Dept C	Philanthropies
Funds available	50	40	20	20	20	20
Required matching contribution (percent)	0%	10%	0%	25%	20%	0%
Will pay matching contribution?	Yes	No	No	No	No	Yes

- There is a set of rules that indicates whether or not COAs are eligible for funding from any given funder. "OK" in the matrix below indicates that they are eligible, and "X" that they are not.

	CDBG-DR	PA	Dept A	Dept B	Dept C	Philanthropies
COA 1	OK	**X**	**X**	OK	OK	OK
COA 2	OK	**X**	OK	**X**	OK	OK
COA 3	OK	OK	OK	**X**	**X**	**X**
COA 4	OK	OK	**X**	**X**	**X**	OK
COA 5	OK	OK	**X**	**X**	**X**	**X**

The problem is to allocate funds so that all COAs are fully funded and all constraints on funder/COA eligibility, and matching-contribution requirements and payments, are met. Since total funding is more than total COA cost, the only problem is to ensure that all the constraints are met.

There are many solutions to this problem; one is

Match	0	10	0	25	20	0		
	CDBG-DR	PA	Dept A	Dept B	Dept C	Philanthropies	SPENT	**COA cost**
COA 1	2.5	**X**	**X**	7.5	0	0	10	10
COA 2	4	**X**	0	**X**	16	0	20	20
COA 3	10	0	20	**X**	**X**	**X**	30	30
COA 4	20	0	**X**	**X**	**X**	20	40	40
COA 5	10	40	**X**	**X**	**X**	**X**	50	50
SPENT	46.5	40	20	7.5	16	20	**150**	150
Funder Budget	50	40	20	20	20	20		

The entries corresponding to each funder/COA combination are spending by that funder on that COA. The "X" entries are retained from the constraint matrix; they illustrate that no ineligible funder/COA combinations are included. The *column* labeled "SPENT" shows the total amount spent on each COA; and the column to its right shows total COA cost. All COAs are fully funded. The *row* labeled "SPENT" shows total spending by each funder; and the row below it shows the funder's budget.

Another solution is

Match	0	10	0	25	20	0		
	CDBG-DR	PA	Dept A	Dept B	Dept C	Philanthropies	SPENT	**COA cost**
COA 1	0	**X**	**X**	7.5	0	2.5	10	10
COA 2	0	**X**	0	**X**	16	4	20	20
COA 3	3	7	20	**X**	**X**	**X**	30	30
COA 4	4	26	**X**	**X**	**X**	10	40	40
COA 5	43	7	**X**	**X**	**X**	**X**	50	50
SPENT	50	40	20	7.5	16	16.5	**150**	150
Funder Budget	50	40	20	20	20	20		

This solution contains more partial funding of COAs by different funders than does the previous solution. Again, in this formulation of the problem there is no restriction on the number of primary funders of any given COA and cost category combination, so long as no primary funder funds more than its own maximum share of the total cost, $m(r, j, f)$, and matching-contribution funds are found for all, which is the case here.

Appendix Summary

This appendix has presented a formal mathematical programming approach to funding analysis. The approach would require (1) a set of COAs, each with a set of costs in various categories; (2) a set of funders, each with a total budget; (3) a set of rules that indicates, for each COA and cost category combination, whether it is eligible or not for funding from any given funder; (4) a set of matching contribution requirements for each funder; and (5) a set of rules on whether each funder will or will not pay matching share requirements.

A programming approach answers the following questions: Is there an allocation of funders to COA and cost category combinations so that all COA costs are covered? If not, what is the best we can do, given a value function over COA achievement (i.e., funding a portion of a cost category for any COA)? We also discussed improvements upon this basic model to account for real-world issues.

4. Summary and Conclusions

Two critical components of a disaster recovery plan are cost and funding analysis. Puerto Rico's recovery plan comprises 276 COAs that are recovery activities designed to redress the hurricane damage and preexisting economic needs faced by Puerto Rico.

Cost analysis consists of estimating the cost associated with carrying out each COA. Such COA-specific cost estimates (developed using a standard set of rules) and cross-COA comparisons can directly support prioritization of resources. *Funding analysis* consists of identifying potential funders who may support the COAs. This can provide a road map for future funding needs in supplemental disaster relief appropriations or ongoing federal agency programs; in addition, it may identify needs that align with areas of interest and capabilities of nongovernmental sources, such as private-sector funding (including P3s) and philanthropic actors. As such, it can provide guidance to those responsible for finding funding for the plan.

Cost Analysis

The primary challenge of the cost analysis was the sheer number and diversity of the COAs included in the plan. The goal of the costing work was to estimate the costs of COAs in a consistent way so that the relative resource challenges of the various COAs were faithfully represented—that is, so that subsequent analysis and selection of COAs for the portfolios ultimately included in Puerto Rico's recovery plan could be done on a consistent cost basis. We developed general ground rules for cost estimation to ensure consistency of the estimates. These included broadly dividing costs into *upfront* and *recurring* costs, selecting a common time horizon for estimating costs, estimating all costs in constant dollar terms, and, where feasible, using standard unit costs—such as labor rates, construction and materials costs, and O&M costs.

We attacked this problem using a diverse set of resources and SMEs, including our own HSOAC expertise; FEMA and other U.S. government personnel; cognizant governmental and nongovernmental entities in Puerto Rico; and subcontractors we specifically engaged for this purpose. We also relied on publicly available federal resources and private commercial cost estimation software and reference materials in consultation with the SMEs.

We used a decentralized approach to cost estimation, whereby sectors individually chose the cost estimation approach they judged most appropriate given the information available—subject to the ground rules, such as common time horizon and labor cost factors, mentioned in Chapter 2. This choice was based on the substantial number of COAs, their sectoral specificity, the technical complexity of infrastructure and other investments, and the great diversity of the activities included in the recovery plan. We judged that, based on these factors, any benefits from a centralized approach would be small compared with the benefits from the in-depth specific sectoral knowledge a decentralized approach could bring to bear.

One common practice across all the sectors was that all the cost estimates were exposed to as wide a set of SMEs as possible for review and comment. Circulation specifically included cognizant persons in Puerto Rico, both in and out of government; FEMA personnel and other CONUS-based persons working on the ground in Puerto Rico; and all cognizant U.S. government agencies. All of this was in addition to HSOAC's formal quality assurance process for review, as well as the fact that a draft of the recovery plan was released to the public on July 9, 2018, for comment.[1]

In this report we have illustrated many of the complexities associated with estimating the costs of a recovery plan. In practical terms, actual recovery plan cost estimates may have to be done in a simpler way because data, or time and resources, do not exist to support more detailed estimation. This is illustrated with examples of our cost estimation for Puerto Rico's recovery plan. Further research into cost estimation methodologies incorporating some of the complexities we could not address in this report would have high value for future disaster recovery work.

Funding Analysis

We have identified potential funders for disaster recovery and discussed a framework for allocating funding sources to individual COAs in Puerto Rico's recovery plan. We considered differing levels of detail in doing a funding analysis. We first identified potential funding sources and the dollar value of their contribution to the recovery plan. Then we more specifically identified potential funding sources for each COA.

The primary funding sources identified include federal government sources, such as the DRF, other appropriations made for disaster relief in legislation, and regular ongoing federal programs. A very high level (99.2 percent) of the total cost of the recovery plan is *eligible* for federal funding, but a gap remains between our estimate of potential federal funding available ($85.6 billion) and funds required to implement the recovery plan ($139 billion). Proceeds from private insurance ($8 billion) will also cover some costs. Additional funding contributions will come from Puerto Rican governmental entities, at either the commonwealth or municipal level, and proceeds from COAs that are revenue-generating projects. Some funders, particularly certain federal programs, will fund only a percentage of any project and require a matching contribution. As such, many COAs will necessarily have more than one funder.

While their levels are currently uncertain, contributions will also come from nongovernmental sources, such as private-sector funding and philanthropic actors. Some investors already figure prominently in natural disaster response, recovery, and mitigation. However, several factors may be stifling greater participation by certain classes of investors; these include a lack of alignment

---

[1] Central Office of Recovery, Reconstruction, and Resiliency, 2018.

with strategic or institutional goals, political and governance risks, and risk-return ratios for recovery and resilience projects. P3s can be a viable way of injecting immediate resources into much-needed infrastructure projects, adding financial flexibility and bringing corporate innovation and technology. However, there may be limitations to P3 due to project feasibility, lack of transparency, poor cost sharing and risk sharing, and imprecise revenue projections.

While philanthropic actors will not cover most of the costs, they may identify specific needs that align with their interests and capabilities to make a meaningful contribution to disaster recovery. For example, one area where charitable foundations can have a major impact is in efforts to build more resilient communities and develop sustainable infrastructure. Corporate giving in the face of natural disasters has increased in the last decade and can take the form of cash, supplies, or coordination of employees as volunteers or targeted problem solvers.

Finally, we discussed construction of a complete funding plan, which would identify specific funders and their contribution to each COA. We judged, and FEMA concurred, that constructing such a plan would not be useful at this early stage of the recovery process. One reason is the large gap between estimated plan cost and funding amounts currently identified. Allocating the funding available would necessarily fund only a subset of the total plan, which would require an assessment (at least implicit) of the relative value of COAs. We had no basis on which do so; the plan was designed as an integral whole.

We described a formal programming approach to funding analysis that addresses the following questions: Is there an allocation of funders to COAs so that all COA costs are covered? And, if not, what is the best option, given a value function over COA achievement (i.e., amount spent, by cost type, on each COA)? We expect that this approach would be a useful tool as the plan is being implemented in the future.

References

100 Resilient Cities, "About Us," webpage, undated. As of February 19, 2019: http://www.100resilientcities.org/about-us/

———, "How to Get Involved," Medium, June 19, 2018. As of November 8, 2018: https://medium.com/urban-resilience-prospectus-latin-america-and-the/how-to-get-involved-ad5b57420160

Abate, Douglas, Michael Towers, Richard Dotz, Luca Romani, and Peter S. Lufkin, *The Whitestone Facility Maintenance and Repair Cost Reference 2009–2010*, Santa Barbara, Calif.: Whitestone Research, 2009.

AbbVie, "AbbVie Donates $100 Million to Strengthen Access to Healthcare, Housing for Hurricane-Ravaged Puerto Rico," May 22, 2018. As of November 8, 2018: https://news.abbvie.com/news/press-releases/abbvie-donates-100-million-to-strengthen-access-to-healthcare-housing-for-hurricane-ravaged-puerto-rico.htm

Acosta, Joie D., Anita Chandra, and Jeanne Ringel, "Nongovernmental Resources to Support Disaster Preparedness, Response and Recovery," *Disaster Medicine and Public Health Preparedness*, Vol. 7, No. 4, August 2013, pp. 348–353.

AIR Worldwide, "AIR Updates Insured Loss Estimates for Hurricane Maria," Press Release, Boston, December 6, 2017. As of May 19, 2019: https://www.air-worldwide.com/Press-Releases/AIR-Updates-Insured-Loss-Estimates-for-Hurricane-Maria/

An, Vickie, "Small Donation, Big Impact: What You Need to Know About Microgiving," *Forbes*, November 13, 2015. As of November 8, 2018: https://www.forbes.com/sites/learnvest/2015/11/13/small-donation-big-impact-what-you-need-to-know-about-microgiving/#73cf03372a36

Belanger, Julie, David Sharrock, Hiroko Araki, Tensai Asfaw, David Matern, Silvanus Okumu, Ekaterina Papaioannou, Lisbeth Pilegaard, and Siti Kamariah Ahmad Subki, *High-Level Panel on Humanitarian Financing: Too Important to Fail—Addressing the Humanitarian Financing Gap*, New York: United Nations, January 2016. As of November 8, 2018: https://reliefweb.int/sites/reliefweb.int/files/resources/%5BHLP%20Report%5D%20Too%20important%20to%20fail%E2%80%94addressing%20the%20humanitarian%20financing%20gap.pdf

Beltrán, Isabel, "One Year Later: The Critical Role of NGOs in Puerto Rico's Recovery," 100 Resilient Cities, September 20, 2018. As of March 1, 2019: https://www.100resilientcities.org/one-year-later-critical-role-ngos-puerto-ricos-recovery/

Bipartisan Policy Center, *Bridging the Gap Together: A New Model to Modernize U.S. Infrastructure*, Washington, D.C.: Bipartisan Policy Center, May 2016. As of March 1, 2019: http://cdn.bipartisanpolicy.org/wp-content/uploads/2016/05/BPC-New-Infrastructure-Model.pdf

BLUEtide Initiative, homepage, undated. As of May 4, 2019: http://bluetidepr.org/index.html

Boynton, Christine, "Aerostar Airport Holdings Wins Bid for San Juan Airport," *Air Transport World*, July 24, 2012. As of May 11, 2018: http://atwonline.com/airports-amp-routes/aerostar-airport-holdings-wins-bid-san-juan-airport

Breitenbach, Sarah, "Nonprofits Poised for Bigger Role in Disaster Recovery," Pew Charitable Trusts, June 23, 2017. As of November 8, 2018: http://www.pewtrusts.org/en/research-and-analysis/blogs/stateline/2017/06/23/nonprofits-poised-for-bigger-role-in-disaster-recovery

Business Civic Leadership Center, *Business Disaster Assistance and Recovery, Second Report: Long-Term Recovery Issues and Case Studies*, Washington, D.C.: Business Civic Leadership Center, August 2007. As of November 8, 2018: https://www.uschamberfoundation.org/sites/default/files/publication/ccc/disasterrecoveryreport0708.pdf

Cambridge Systematics, *Rural Interstate Corridor Communications Study: Report to States*, Washington, D.C.: Federal Highway Administration, February 2009. As of May 5, 2019: https://ops.fhwa.dot.gov/publications/fhwahop09021/fhwahop09021.pdf

Capps, Kriston, "How Local Governments Came to Embrace Business Partnerships," CityLab, November 10, 2017. As of November 8, 2018: https://www.citylab.com/solutions/2017/11/local-governments-partner-with-business/542487/

Cario, Cindy, Andrew Grabois, Naomi Henry, Supriya Kumar, Lawrence T. McGill, Darya Oreshkina, Betty Saronson, Grace Sato, Kathy Gutowsky, Robert G. Ottenhoff, and Regine A. Webster, *Measuring the State of Disaster Philanthropy*, New York: Foundation Center and Center for Disaster Philanthropy, 2017. As of November 8, 2018: https://www.issuelab.org/resources/28353/28353.pdf

CBRE Business Analytics, "CostLab," webpage, undated. As of May 6, 2019: https://www.cbre.com/real-estate-services/occupier/client-strategy-and-consulting/cbre-business-analytics/costlab

Çelik, Serdar, and Mats Isaksson, "Institutional Investors and Ownership Engagement," *OECD Journal: Financial Market Trends*, Vol. 2013, No. 2, 2014. As of December 8, 2018: https://www.oecd.org/corporate/Institutional-investors-ownership-engagement.pdf

Central Office of Recovery, Reconstruction, and Resiliency, "Transformation and Innovation in the Wake of Devastation: An Economic and Disaster Recovery Plan for Puerto Rico," San Juan, P.R.: Central Office of Recovery, Reconstruction, and Resiliency, July 9, 2018, preliminary draft manuscript. As of April 29, 2019: http://www.p3.pr.gov/assets/pr-draft-recovery-plan-for-comment-july-9-2018.pdf

Chandra, Anita, and Joie Acosta, *The Role of Nongovernmental Organizations in Long-Term Human Recovery After Disaster: Reflections from Louisiana Four Years After Hurricane Katrina*, Santa Monica, Calif.: RAND Corporation, OP-277-RC, 2009. As of May 5, 2019: https://www.rand.org/pubs/occasional_papers/OP277.html

Clontz, Brian, Doug Stockham, and Ryan Raffin, "Lessons Learned from Recent Natural Disaster Relief Funds: Part 1 of 3," Planned Giving Design Center, April 21, 2015. As of November 8, 2018: https://www.pgdc.com/pgdc/lessons-learned-recent-natural-disaster-relief-funds-part-1-3

DHS—*See* U.S. Department of Homeland Security.

Disaster Recovery Network at GlobalGiving, "Puerto Rico & Caribbean Hurricane Relief Fund," GlobalGiving, undated. As of March 1, 2019: https://www.globalgiving.org/projects/hurricane-maria-caribbean-relief-fund/

Estudios Técnicos Inc., *Snapshot of Federal Assistance Programs FY 2010*, Commonwealth of Puerto Rico, Office of Management and Budget, December 2013. As of May 19, 2019: https://estadisticas.pr/files/BibliotecaVirtual/estadisticas/biblioteca/OGP_Snapshot_of_Federal_Assistance_Programs_FY2010_2013.pdf

"Extreme Conditions Spur Innovative Community Response," Unidos por Puerto Rico, February 20, 2019. As of March 1, 2019: https://www.unidosporpuertorico.com/extreme-conditions-spur-innovative-community-response/

Federal Emergency Management Agency, "National Disaster Recovery Framework," webpage, undated. As of May 7, 2019: https://www.fema.gov/national-disaster-recovery-framework

———, "FEMA-4339-DR, Puerto Rico Disaster Declaration as of 11/01/2017," webpage, 2017. As of April 24, 2018: https://gis.fema.gov/maps/dec_4339.pdf

———, *Public Assistance Program and Policy Guide*, Washington, D.C.: Federal Emergency Management Agency, FP 104-009-2, April 2018. As of March 12, 2019: https://www.fema.gov/media-library-data/1525468328389-4a038bbef9081cd7dfe7538e7751aa9c/PAPPG_3.1_508_FINAL_5-4-2018.pdf

Federal Highway Administration, Center for Innovative Finance Support, "Project Profile: Puerto Rico PR-22 and PR-5 Lease," undated. As of May 15, 2018: https://www.fhwa.dot.gov/ipd/project_profiles/pr_pr22_and_pr5_lease.aspx

Federal Transit Administration, *The Predicted and Actual Impacts of New Starts Projects—2007: Capital Cost and Ridership*, Washington, D.C.: Federal Transit Administration, April 2008.

FEMA—*See* Federal Emergency Management Agency.

Financial Oversight and Management Board for Puerto Rico, *New Fiscal Plan for Puerto Rico: Restoring Growth and Prosperity*, San Juan, P.R.: Financial Oversight and Management Board for Puerto Rico, May 30, 2018. As of May 5, 2019: https://drive.google.com/file/d/1eHZ1_lM7Cb4yw_hrI_Ju-vW6Yd1kD2_k/view

Ford Foundation, "Foundations Commit $5M to Ensure an Equitable Recovery in Puerto Rico," New York, November 16, 2017. As of February 19, 2019: https://www.fordfoundation.org/the-latest/news/foundations-commit-5m-to-ensure-an-equitable-recovery-in-puerto-rico/

Foundation for Puerto Rico, "Foundation for Puerto Rico Hurricane Maria Relief Fund," webpage, undated. As of March 1, 2019: https://www.foundationforpuertorico.org/hurricane-efforts

Gates, Bill, "Why Inequality Matters," Gatesnotes: The Blog of Bill Gates, October 13, 2014. As of November 8, 2018: https://www.gatesnotes.com/Books/Why-Inequality-Matters-Capital-in-21st-Century-Review

Gbadebo-Smith, Orinola, "The Wealth of Nations: Investment Strategies of Sovereign Wealth Funds," Toptal, undated. As of December 8, 2018: https://www.toptal.com/finance/market-rsearch-analysts/sovereign-wealth-funds

The Giving Pledge, "A Commitment to Philanthropy," homepage, undated. As of November 8, 2018: https://givingpledge.org/Home.aspx

Giving USA, *Giving USA 2018: The Annual Report on Philanthropy for the Year 2017*, Chicago: Giving USA Foundation and Indiana University Purdue University Indianapolis Lilly Family School of Philanthropy, 2018.

Government of Puerto Rico, *New Fiscal Plan for Puerto Rico*, San Juan, P.R.: Government of Puerto Rico, April 5, 2018. As of May 19, 2019: http://www.aafaf.pr.gov/assets/newfiscalplanforpuerto-rico-2018-04-05.pdf

Government of Puerto Rico, *Transformation and Innovation in the Wake of Devastation: An Economic and Disaster Recovery Plan for Puerto Rico*, San Juan, P.R.: Government of Puerto Rico, August 8, 2018. As of April 10, 2019: http://www.p3.pr.gov/assets/ pr-transformation-innovation-plan-congressional-submission-080818.pdf

Government of Puerto Rico, Office of the Governor, Planning Board, *Apéndice Estadístico / Statistical Appendix*, San Juan, P.R.: Government of Puerto Rico, 2016. As of May 5, 2019: http://www.aafaf.pr.gov/spanish/assets/apendiceestadistico2016.pdf

Government of Puerto Rico, Puerto Rico Public-Private Partnership Authority, "Inventory of Projects," webpage, undated. As of February 19, 2019: http://www.p3.pr.gov/inventory-of-projects.html

Grogan, T., and W. J. Angelo, "Katrina Gives Inflation a Second Wind," *ENR Cost Report*, 3Q (2005), pp. 66–68.

Henderson, Liz, "The Role of Insurance in Building Resilience," Aon, undated. As of May 4, 2019: https://www.aon.com/reinsurance/gimo/20180911-gimo-protection-gap?utm_source =slipcase&utm_medium=affiliate&utm_campaign=slipcase

Horrocks, Paul, Wiebke Bartz-Zuccala, Irene Basile, Naeeda Crishna Morgado, Jens Sedemund, Julia Benn, Cécile Sangare, and Tomas Hos, *Blended Finance: Mobilising Resources for Sustainable Development and Climate Action in Developing Countries*, Paris: Organisation for Economic Co-operation and Development, October 2017. As of November 8, 2018: https://www.oecd.org/cgfi/forum/Blended-finance-Policy-Perspectives.pdf

HUD—*See* U.S. Department of Housing and Urban Development.

Hull, Pete, Stephen Bowen, Tanya Buttress, Bridget Kanawati, Russell Miller, Richard Rowe, Sarah Maloney, and John Sopko, *Heralding Unheard Voices: The Role of Faith-Based Organizations and Nongovernmental Organizations During Disasters, Final Report*, Arlington, Va.: Homeland Security Institute, December 18, 2006. As of November 8, 2018: https://ntrl.ntis.gov/NTRL/dashboard/searchResults/titleDetail/PB2010103566.xhtml

Ivanova, Iliana, Oskar Herics, Thomas Obermayr, Pietro Puricella, Enrico Grassi, Guido Fara, Di Hai, Svetoslav Hristov, Maria Carmen Jiménez, Chrysoula Latopoulou, and Maria Ploumaki, *Public Private Partnerships in the EU: Widespread Shortcomings and Limited Benefits*, Luxembourg: European Court of Auditors, European Union, 2018. As of November 8, 2018: https://www.eca.europa.eu/Lists/ECADocuments/SR18_09/SR_PPP_EN.pdf

KPMG LLP, *The American National Red Cross: Consolidated Financial Statements*, McLean, Va.: KPMG LLP, June 30, 2015. As of November 8, 2018: https://www.redcross.org/content/dam/redcross/enterprise-assets/pdfs/m56240343_2015_TheAmericanNationalRedCross_CFS.PDF

Leonard, Devin, "'The Only Lifeline Was the Wal-Mart,'" *Fortune*, October 3, 2005, pp. 74–80. As of November 8, 2018: http://archive.fortune.com/magazines/fortune/fortune_archive/2005/10/03/8356743/index.htm

McCarthy, Kevin F., *An Economic Development Architecture for New Orleans*, Santa Monica, Calif.: RAND Corporation, TR-547-HI, 2008. As of November 8, 2018: https://www.rand.org/pubs/technical_reports/TR547.html

Monllor, Javier, and Nezih Altay, "Discovering Opportunities in Necessity: The Inverse Creative Destruction Effect," *Journal of Small Business and Enterprise Development*, Vol. 23, No. 1, 2016, pp. 274–291.

Morain, Tony, "Direct Relief, Merck and Partners Test Temperature-Controlled Autonomous Drone Delivery System for Medicines in Puerto Rico," Direct Relief, August 24, 2018. As of March 1, 2019: https://www.directrelief.org/2018/08/direct-relief-merck-and-partners-test-temperature-controlled-autonomous-drone-delivery-system-for-medicines-in-puerto-rico/

Moselle, Ben, ed., *Craftsman 2018 National Building Cost Manual*, Carlsbad, Calif.: Craftsman Book Company, 2017.

Muller, Alan, and Gail Whiteman, "Exploring the Geography of Corporate Philanthropic Disaster Response: A Study of Fortune Global 500 Firms," *Journal of Business Ethics*, Vol. 84, No. 4, 2009, pp. 589–603.

Nason, Sara, *One Year Later: Hurricane Maria*, Glen Rock, N.J.: Charity Navigator, 2018. As of March 1, 2019: https://s3.amazonaws.com/cn-web-site/Charity+Navigator's+Hurricane+Maria+Study.pdf

National Philanthropic Trust, "Charitable Giving Statistics," webpage, undated. As of November 8, 2018: https://www.nptrust.org/philanthropic-resources/charitable-giving-statistics/

Nonprofit Action, "Facts and Stats About NGOs Worldwide," webpage, September 4, 2015. As of November 8, 2018: http://nonprofitaction.org/2015/09/facts-and-stats-about-ngos-worldwide/

NRICH Team, "Clever Carl," NRICH, webpage, last updated September 2012. As of May 6, 2019: https://nrich.maths.org/2478

Oppenheim, Jeremy, and Katherine Stodulka, "Mobilizing Private Infrastructure for Sustainable Finance," paper presented at the Business and Sustainable Development Coalition G20 Brainstorming Workshop, Buenos Aires, September 2017. As of May 5, 2019: https://www.brookings.edu/wp-content/uploads/2017/11/mobilizing-private-finance-for-sustainable-infrastructure-brief.pdf

Osa, Yukie, "The Growing Role of NGOs in Disaster Relief and Humanitarian Assistance in East Asia," in Rizal Sukma and James Gannon, eds., *A Growing Force: Civil Society's Role in Asian Regional Security*, Tokyo: Japan Center for International Exchange, 2013, pp. 66–89. As of May 4, 2019: http://www.jcie.org/researchpdfs/growingforce/5_Osa.pdf

Painter, William L., *2017 Disaster Supplemental Appropriations: Overview*, Washington, D.C.: Congressional Research Service, January 25, 2018. As of May 4, 2019: https://www.hsdl.org/?view&did=807909

Peters, Adele, "During Puerto Rico's Blackout, Solar Microgrids Kept the Lights On," *Fast Company*, April 24, 2018. As of March 1, 2019: https://www.fastcompany.com/40562660/during-puerto-ricos-blackout-solar-microgrids-kept-the-lights-on

Plyer, Allison, Nihal Shrinath, and Vicki Mack, "The New Orleans Index at Ten: Measuring Greater New Orleans' Progress Toward Prosperity," The Data Center, July 31, 2015. As of November 8, 2018: https://www.datacenterresearch.org/reports_analysis/new-orleans-index-at-ten/

Puerto Rico Department of Economic Development and Commerce, "Governor of Puerto Rico Declared the Island 'Open for Business,' and Invited Investors and Entrepreneurs to Be Part of Its Economic Transformation," Business Wire, February 15, 2018. As of February 19, 2019: https://www.businesswire.com/news/home/20180215005585/en/Governor-Puerto-Rico-Declared-Island-%E2%80%9COpen-Business%E2%80%9D

RAND Corporation, "Supporting Puerto Rico's Disaster-Recovery Planning," webpage, undated. As of May 4, 2019: http://www.rand.org/hsoac/puerto-rico-recovery

Raymond, Hélène, "Sovereign Wealth Funds as Domestic Investors of Last Resort During Crises," *International Economics / Economie Internationale*, Vol. 123, 2010, pp. 121–159. As of December 8, 2018: https://www.cairn.info/revue-economie-internationale-2010-3-page-121.htm

Raymond, Susan U., *Recession, Recovery, and Renewal: Long-Term Nonprofit Strategies for Rapid Economic Change*, Hoboken, N.J.: John Wiley and Sons, 2013.

Rock, Edward B. "Institutional Investors in Corporate Governance," University of Pennsylvania Law School, Faculty Scholarship Paper 1458, July 21, 2015. As of December 8, 2018: https://scholarship.law.upenn.edu/cgi/viewcontent.cgi?article=2459&context=faculty_scholarship

RSMeans, homepage, undated. As of May 6, 2019: https://www.rsmeans.com

S.B. 469, Act No. 29, Public-Private Partnerships Act of Puerto Rico, Government Bank of Puerto Rico, June 8, 2009. As of May 7, 2019: http://www.gdb-pur.com/publications-reports/documents/2009-06-08-APPs-ing.pdf

Semler, P. K., "Puerto Rico Becomes Pilot for Trump's $1.5Tn P3 Fund," *Asia Times*, July 2, 2018. As of May 4, 2019: https://www.asiatimes.com/2018/07/opinion/puerto-rico-becomes-pilot-for-trumps-1-5tn-p3-fund/

Stys, Jeffrey J., "Non-Profit Involvement in Disaster Response and Recovery," paper prepared for the Center for Law, Environment, Adaptation and Resources, University of North Carolina School of Law, January 17, 2011. As of November 8, 2018: http://www.law.unc.edu/documents/clear/publications/nonprofit.pdf

Thorpe, Devin, "In Under 60 Days, Crowdfunding Sites Raise over $20 Million for Nepal Relief," *Forbes*, June 12, 2015. As of November 8, 2018: https://www.forbes.com/sites/devinthorpe/2015/06/12/in-under-60-days-crowdfunding-sites-raise-over-20-million-for-nepal-relief/#3f5daf128a4d

Tresise, Caroline Baxter, "How Entrepreneurship Can Support Post-Disaster Recovery," Oxfam, May 25, 2017. As of November 8, 2018: https://views-voices.oxfam.org.uk/general/2017/05/entrepreneurship-can-support-post-disaster-recovery

Truman, Edwin M., *Sovereign Wealth Funds: Threat or Salvation?* Washington, D.C.: Peterson Institute for International Economics, 2010.

Unidos por Puerto Rico, "Donations in Action," webpage, undated. As of February 19, 2019: https://www.unidosporpuertorico.com/accountability/

U.S. Bureau of Economic Analysis, "Industry Data," web database, undated. As of May 4, 2019: https://www.bea.gov/iTable/iTable.cfm?ReqID=51&step=1#reqid=51&step=2&isuri=1

———, "Gross Domestic Product, Third Quarter 2018 (Third Estimate); Corporate Profits, Third Quarter 2018 (Revised Estimate)," Washington, D.C., December 21, 2018. As of May 6, 2019: https://www.bea.gov/system/files/2018-12/gdp3q18_3rd_1.pdf

U.S. Bureau of Labor Statistics, "May 2017 State Occupational Employment and Wage Estimates: Puerto Rico," web database, last modified March 30, 2018a. As of May 5, 2019: https://www.bls.gov/oes/2017/may/oes_pr.htm

———, *Occupational Outlook Handbook*, 2018–2019 ed., Lanham, Md.: Bernan Press, 2018b.

U.S. Census Bureau, *Federal Aid to States for Fiscal Year 2010*, Washington, D.C.: U.S. Government Printing Office, September 2011.

U.S. Department of Homeland Security, *National Disaster Recovery Framework*, 2nd ed., Washington, D.C.: U.S. Department of Homeland Security, 2016. As of April 25, 2018: https://www.fema.gov/media-library-data/1466014998123-4bec8550930f774269e0c5968b120ba2/National_Disaster_Recovery_Framework2nd.pdf

U.S. Department of Housing and Urban Development, "HUD Awards $28 Billion in CDBG-DR Funds," Washington, D.C.: April 11, 2018a. As of May 7, 2019: https://www.hudexchange.info/news/hud-awards-28-billion-in-cdbg-dr-funds/

———, "HUD and Puerto Rico Ink $1.5 Billion Disaster Recovery Grant Agreement," Washington, D.C., September 20, 2018. As of May 7, 2019: https://www.hud.gov/press/press_releases_media_advisories/HUD_No_18_104

U.S. Department of Transportation, "Port of Miami Tunnel," webpage, undated. As of March 1, 2019: https://www.transportation.gov/tifia/financed-projects/port-miami-tunnel

———, "Teodoro Moscoso Bridge, San Juan, Puerto Rico," webpage, last updated September 9, 2014. As of May 15, 2018: https://www.transportation.gov/policy-initiatives/build-america/teodoro-moscoso-bridge-san-juan-puerto-rico

U.S. Department of the Treasury, "Treasury, IRS Announce First Round of Opportunity Zones Designations for 18 States," Washington, D.C., April 9, 2018. As of February 19, 2019: https://home.treasury.gov/news/press-releases/sm0341

U.S. General Services Administration, *2018 Catalog of Federal Domestic Assistance*, Washington, D.C.: U.S. General Services Administration, November 2018. As of May 5, 2019: https://api.sam.gov/prod/fac/v1/programs/downloadPublication/2018?api_key=O4kzViWGVYNumPqhAzUhYGiZZZwW3RKUEYJOI6ii

U.S. Government Accountability Office, *Airport Privatization: Limited Interest Despite FAA's Pilot Program*, Washington, D.C.: U.S. Government Accountability Office, GAO-15-42, November 2014.

U.S. Senate Committee on Appropriations, *Supplemental Appropriations for Disaster Relief and Recovery*, Washington, D.C.: U.S. Senate Committee on Appropriations, undated. As of May 4, 2019:
https://www.appropriations.senate.gov/imo/media/doc/020718-SUPPLEMENTAL-SUMMARY.pdf

U.S. Trust, *The 2016 U.S. Trust Study of High Net Worth Philanthropy: Charitable Practices and Preferences of Wealthy Households*, New York: U.S. Trust and Indiana University Lilly Family School of Philanthropy, October 2016. As of November 8, 2018:
https://www.ustrust.com/publish/content/application/pdf/GWMOL/USTp_ARMCGDN7_oct_2017.pdf

Villafañe, Veronica, "Jennifer Lopez, Daddy Yankee Donate $1 Million to Puerto Rico; Maná Gives $200,000 to Aid Mexico," *Forbes*, September 25, 2017. As of March 1, 2019:
https://www.forbes.com/sites/veronicavillafane/2017/09/25/jennifer-lopez-daddy-yankee-donate-1-million-to-puerto-rico-mana-gives-200000-to-aid-mexico/#6ef3b9925ff6

Weinstein, Stanley, and Pamela Barden, *The Complete Guide to Fundraising Management*, 4th ed., Hoboken, N.J.: John Wiley and Sons, 2017.

Westgarth, Alastair, "Turning on Project Loon in Puerto Rico," Medium, October 20, 2017. As of March 1, 2019:
https://medium.com/loon-for-all/turning-on-project-loon-in-puerto-rico-f3aa41ad2d7f

Zimmerman, Ann, and Valerie Bauerlein, "At Wal-Mart, Emergency Plan Has Big Payoff," *Wall Street Journal*, September 12, 2005. As of November 8, 2018:
http://www.wsj.com/articles/SB112648681539237605

Zinsmeister, Karl, "The Philanthropy of the Little Guys," *World*, March 10, 2018. As of November 8, 2018:
https://world.wng.org/content/the_philanthropy_of_the_little_guys